LIVE.

A Spiritual and

LEARN.

Personal Growth Journey

GROW.

DEDRA D. COLSTON

WESTBOW
PRESS®
A DIVISION OF THOMAS NELSON
& ZONDERVAN

Scripture taken from the Amplified Bible, Copyright © 1954, 1958, 1962, 1964, 1965, 1987 by The Lockman Foundation. Used with permission.

WestBow Press books may be ordered through booksellers or by contacting:

WestBow Press
A Division of Thomas Nelson & Zondervan
1663 Liberty Drive
Bloomington, IN 47403
www.westbowpress.com
1 (866) 928-1240

ISBN: 978-1-9736-1738-9 (sc)
ISBN: 978-1-9736-1740-2 (hc)
ISBN: 978-1-9736-1739-6 (e)

Library of Congress Control Number: 2018901256

Print information available on the last page.

WestBow Press rev. date: 03/30/2018

A WORD OF THANKS

Thank you for purchasing "Live. Learn. Grow: A spiritual and personal growth journey". I pray that you will be able to make connections and grow during this devotional. Each section was inspired by God and I pray you will be blessed. Thank you for intentionally setting aside time to connect with God on purpose. I pray that you are able to hear God through the stories and connect with Him during reflection time. Thank you for reaching deep to ask yourself the hard questions in order to mature in your spiritual walk. I pray that if this devotional is a blessing to you, that you will pay it forward and tell someone else who needs or wants to grow in their spiritual journey. All of our journeys are different, but if we look deeper, they all bring us back to our Savior! Thank you for taking the plunge to understand yourself and your relationship with God. I pray that from this moment you will continue on your journey of growth, because our spiritual growth is never complete because there is always more to learn when new challenges arise; but I pray that you will this time choose the option of picking up your basic instructions before leaving earth, your BIBLE, and dig in to get the answers, encouragement, inspiration and motivation that you need. Blessings and prosperity to you on your journey! - Dedra

~Dad~

I would like to thank my father, Michael Colston for being the priest of our family. Dad thank you for ensuring that we were properly taught the word of God by seeking out a church home that not only fed me the word, but open my spirit up to want more from God. Thank you for praying for me and with me! Thank you for teaching us the word and having bible study with us growing up. Dad, thank you for always giving us a word when we were faced with a challenge whether we wanted to hear it or not, it worked! I thank you for having unconditional love and supporting me in all my endeavors. I know that if no one else supported me you and mom did! Dad, thank you for never giving up on me, for being my sounding board, my agitator and my hero! I know that we bump heads a lot, but we are one in the same! Thank you for loving me like you do, always ready to risk it all! I appreciate each and everything you have done, even when it hurt, it was a lesson learned and taught me more about myself and the love and power of God.

~Mom~

I know many people do not call their mothers their best-friend, but you are my bestie! I love you dearly! Mom, thank you for always going the extra mile and seeking ways of making a connection with me growing up! Thank you for wanting a relationship with me that surpassed a basic mother and daughter relationship. I can truly say that I never had the rebellious stage with you and the all-out fights like some mothers and daughters do. I appreciate you coming to me when I was in middle school asking me what it was that you did that I did not like. That was a wow moment to me! I could not believe my mother actually cared so much. There were ups and downs, but never fall-outs and I am appreciative of that! Thank you for your unfailing support and listening ear! Thank you for being my nurse, personal shopper and tear wiper! You have seen me at my worst and still love me and I thank you for that! Thank you for telling me that I can do it and believing in the vision God has given me. Thank you for tagging along and helping me be obedient to God, because in that you were blessed too! Thank for you never giving up on me and encouraging me when I am low. You are truly my BFF (best friend forever) and I could not ask for more!

INTRODUCTION

Have you ever wondered why you are here or what your existence truly means? What about those things that come naturally to you like dancing, speaking, writing, drawing, creating, invocating passion and drive in others; what are you to do with them and how can they be of help or use to the world in general? What does it all mean and how am I to be effective? We are always in search of answers and reasons, but do we ever stop to think about how we can reach just one person outside of ourselves with those abilities and gifts, or do we try to make it all about us? I believe the latter is true for most in our society. We live for how we can please our flesh. We seldom give thought to using our gifts or talents to improve the quality of life for another human being. We go day to day planning our future and advancements to give us satisfaction never really thinking about how we can plan to help others. At an early age, I realized I had the gift of written expression. Words seemed to come easily to me and my imagination was vast; ever creating scenes. I loved reading, and poetry became an outlet of expression for me. I wrote a book, if you will call it that, in the sixth grade that won me the classroom competition and my parents' awestruck approval and disapproval at the same time. By the time I reached adulthood my writings had matured, and I just knew I wanted to be an author until my small group leader challenged me from church. She asked me what was my gift for and who was to benefit from it? I was naturally confused, because writing "secular" things flowed out of me like water and if it came to me that easily, then it was natural, right? I mean what is wrong with writing about love and the test and trials of relationships?

Well, that day was the beginning of my inner struggle and I began to soul search.

I love God with all my being. I worship and praise him like no other, but the question that had me trapped was," Am I worshipping and praising him with my talent?" I had already begun writing a short story for the concept of the book I was developing when she knocked me down with that question. For two years, I wrote nothing. My drive and desire were gone, and I decided I needed to "grow". I spent the next 2 years growing my relationship with God. I became a small group leader and eventually began writing spiritually based poetry, and then it happened! I finally understood the question. You see, to be a blessing to God we must bless others. My plan of writing and becoming a "secular" author was not going to uplift, motivate, nor bless others. My writing could have given pleasure, but was that the type of pleasure I wanted to create in others. Maturing in your walk is an important aspect of living a Christian life. Each day we live is a learning process and as a result, we grow; and I most definitely grew. I started a Christian blog that not only blessed me, but it blessed and uplifted others. Then I begin to be inundated with inspirational quotes that would drop into my spirit at any given moment, and I begin writing affirmations that led to this idea of Live, Learn, Grow.

When I think about the title, I think about summer and my youth. I always knew summer had arrived when I started to see the floating specks of light in the air. As a child, I called them "lightening bugs". Although they are called fireflies, I will use the term "lightening bugs". Those bugs drew me like bees to a honeycomb. I just had to have them because I wanted my room to glow at night. I vividly remember finding a jar and capturing them. I took special care to punch holes in the lid so that they would survive overnight. I would climb into bed eager and ready to watch them glow and somewhere along the way, I would fall asleep and to my dismay in the morning, I would notice that although I provided them with oxygen they would be dead, and I could not understand why. How could they die when I provided them with oxygen and why was the oxygen I provided not enough? Where did I go wrong? Now, fast forward to adulthood and I began to connect how we are like those "lightening bugs". In life we grow up with dreams, desires and passions; and we feel free. We feel like the world is ours and nothing can stop us, but then it happens, we become encased like the "lightening bugs". We give ourselves just a little room to grow and BAM, FEAR takes over and zaps the life out of us. We die. Our dreams die. Our desires get pushed to the back burner, and we stop living and pressing toward the life we are meant to have. We stop learning more about ourselves, stunt our growth and die on the inside in the process. But, when we are FREE, WILLING, and READY to live our lives, we become like that little "lightening bug". We float, glow, and bring happiness and inspiration to others. Live, Learn, Grow will make you feel good, bad and somewhere in-between. These "nuggets", as I call them, will challenge you in your spiritual walk to grow you so that you will stop living a dead life and learn live a life of fullness solely relying on God. We tend to focus solely on ourselves, what we want, and think is best; and in that forget who is in control and has the master plan.

As you meditate on these "nuggets" begin to work them into your daily living. Write down how you would like to grow and use them each day or week. My desire is that you are pricked with the desire to live a *golden life*, a life of empowerment; conquering the day to day task of living and in the process, help someone else to live a *golden life* as well.

Live have several different meanings, but these are the ones I would like to focus on:

Live

1) to be alive
2) to maintain oneself; subsist
3) to have a life rich in existence
4) to act out, practice

*Merriam-Webster's Dictionary

Out of these definitions, the fourth definition is the one that fits where we will go on this journey of live, learn, grow. We are "caught up" in life and our own existence that we forget how to exist. We forget to live a rich and full life. We forget to live a life of being present and in the moment, and we forget to live a life of giving back and doing for people outside of our immediate circle and self. We live in a culture that has become a selfish one, whereas, a vast majority of us do not seek to help those in need, nor do we do look for opportunities to lift someone else up. Social media has by far taken over everyone's life in some form or fashion. This platform seems to give the sense through photos, postings or snaps that people are living the life only showing us a glimpse of a moment in time. It has birthed a false sense of living so much that people are not living. I have been witnessed to such moments of groups of people sitting quietly and suddenly a "fun and lively" photo is taken and afterwards, everyone goes back to their respective positions and phones with no interaction thereafter. I watch as this goes on and on and this is where we have come. We have come to the perfect photo highlighting just how much fun we are having! However, it is all a façade. We must learn that living and being alive is being in the moment, mindful, present and enjoying it to the fullest. The best days and nights I have had were not captured in a photo, post or snap…you know why? Because I was busy living and all I have to remember the moment is my memory!

Learn: What do we need to learn? What do we do with the information or insight that we have learned?

Learn

1) to gain knowledge or skill by practicing, studying, being taught or experiencing something
2) to find something out
3) to come to realize
4) to come to know
5) to acquire knowledge or skill or behavioral tendency

Merriam-Webster's Dictionary

Life deals in lessons every day that we walk this earth. Some lessons are hard and some we never learn from. We learn things from the time we come out of our mother's womb until the day we take our last breath. Learning is therefore life long, but what happens when we repeat the same lesson(s) repeatedly? Somewhere along the lines, we did not learn from it, even if it left us in despair. Learning is all about opening yourself up to new ideas and experiences to know what is good and beneficial for you. Once you learn these new acquired skills or knowledge, you must begin to expand and grow. When you learn something, it is not just for you, but for others too. We are to share our knowledge with others to help them in their journey of growth and discovery. In my teenage and young adult years, I always told my parents to let me figure things out on my own, and no matter how much they wanted to step in, they respected me and allowed me to make my own mistakes. I wanted to experience the "hiccup" and learn from my mistake. However, when we stop people from experiencing life, they never learn the necessary skills to improve or change course. This "savior behavior" as I call it, dwarfs growth and sets one up for failure. Learning is an essential part of life and although it is not blissful at times, it is always what we need to do in order to mature to the next level of this thing we call life.

Grow- How do we grow and what does it mean in relation to living and learning?

Grow

1) to become better or improved in some way: to become more developed, mature, etc.
2) to become larger and change from being a child to be an adult as time passes: to pass from childhood to adulthood
3) to spring up and develop to maturity
4) to increase, expand (as in wisdom)

Merriam-Webster's Dictionary

In this thing called life, we live and learn daily. Therefore, what do we do with all of our living and learning; we grow! Growth is a beautiful and wonderful thing. I am in awe watching my niece and nephew grow. When I look back at old photos, I sometimes yearn for the days where I could hold them in my arms and inhale that good ole baby smell! As each year passes, I watch their progress and personalities form and become solidified, leaving the former child behind. Growing is an expectation for physical growth, but as we become adults, we sometimes stop growing because life takes over and we go with the flow of it. As children, we have our parents and other adults to help guide and mold us, but as we enter adulthood and move forward on our own, we become responsible for our decisions and spiritual, emotional and mental growth. Some areas we focus on more than others are, but if we never take the time to grow spiritually and find that connectedness; our emotional and mental growth suffers in the end. Living and learning means nothing if we are not growing. As sons and daughters of the King, we cannot live a stagnant life. Our lives have purpose and meaning. When we allow ourselves to live and learn from life's lessons, we grow in wisdom and are able to help others live a life of meaning and purpose.

Remember, your journey in life is to live life to the fullest, learn from your mistakes and life's encounters, and grow from them so that you can be the best you there is.

You only have one life to live. It's high time to make the best of it! – Dedra Colston

It's Time to LIVE

LIVE

You only have one life to live! Live for TODAY! Plan for tomorrow! Do not worry about things you have no control over. Remember you are only here for a moment in space and time. Make the most of it!

Mindfulness is the new counseling term being talked about everywhere. Although this concept has been around for years, it has had a rebirth in recent years. Mindfulness is very simple in theory, but quite hard for us to do. Mindfulness requires one to be present and in the moment. It requires one to acknowledge and be aware of your feelings, emotions, thoughts, and the presence of things and the environment around you. This therapeutic technique simply wants one to slow down and get in touch with their present self. When we are always planning for the next day, week, month and year we forget to be still and present in the now. We have to learn to stop this destructive behavior. When we do not live in the now, we cause unnecessary stress and it robs of us of enjoying or dealing with our current situations. We must learn to "live in the 24"! What is "living in the 24"? Living in the 24 is living, doing, working, learning and growing in one day not the next day or thinking about the next day, but actually being present and connected to what is going on in the now. As a child of God, we have to learn that He has our tomorrow all figured out, and we are simply catching up to it. I am not saying we cannot plan, but when we do, we should always include God in the plan! He says to write the vision and make it plain, but do not let tomorrow overshadow what is going on in the now. Remember it is time to Live!

Reflections:

How can I actively LIVE in the now?

How can practicing mindfulness help me to live in the present?

What steps can I take to help me not worry about tomorrow?

When I begin to stress about the future, what can I do to bring me back to focus on my present and work from there?

Read and meditate on Jeremiah 29:11. What is this verse saying to you? What is being revealed about to you about your relationship with God? How will you begin to allow Jeremiah 29:11 to guide you in your everyday life?

LIVE

A life full of happiness! If things or people take away from your happiness, let it or those people go!

Letting go is hard to do! Sometimes we hold on to things or people because of the comfort or false sense of security. If something is weighing you down and you constantly find yourself sad, stressed and depressed, it's time to set yourself free from it. I was involved with someone for years off and on, crazy, right? I was in love and loved this person and although we had gone our separate ways, I allowed this person to enter at will into my life because of the love I held on to. It was vicious cycles of emotional highs which always left me a total train wreck. I often found myself regretting each time I allowed this person to come back in. I knew in my heart that this was not a good situation for me because I was not wanted in the way I wanted to be. Therefore, I clung to the notion that this person cared for and loved me, so I continued the destructive behavior. Yes, my rationale was hurting me mentally and emotionally, but I continued to allow it. We would have many discussions and for some periods, did not see or talk with one another, but eventually we always came back together for a brief time. It was not until I had a long talk with myself; yes, we need to do that sometimes, and told myself I needed to love someone who loves me the way I love them and with that I let go. Did it hurt? YES. Did I cry for some days? YES, 3 days to be exact (that is the amount of time I gave myself to hurt).

But I realized I was not choosing happiness; I was robbing myself from it. When we hold on to things that are not good for us it becomes toxic; and toxic situation kill your happiness. If you are not receiving what you are giving, it is time to let it go. Whether it is a job or relationship with a significant other or family member, you have to learn to do what is best for you and your health. Having a peace of mind is priceless, so why allow others to destroy that for you? You have to learn to do for you and your well-being first when it comes to your happiness. Does that sound selfish? Yes, it may, but think about it, if you are not doing what makes you happy and brings you peace and joy, will you be good for you or anything else? Will you be emotionally healthy? No, you will not, and the job or other person will keep right on living and existing. Generally speaking, a person usually does not stay at a job for long when they are dissatisfied because they soon become unproductive, miss days and are often sick. But on the opposing side, a person will usually remain in an unhealthy relationship due to self-esteem or familial ties even though it is causing them physical, emotional and mental health problems. Why is that? The job can easily be replaced, or you can find other outlets to de-stress until you move on, but with familial and relational relationships, those ties and bonds are strong, and guilt becomes a main culprit in keeping you in the Death Valley of happiness. Then the question becomes why me? Well only you know when you are ready to choose to let go and be happy! Only you know when you have had enough and want to live a life of peace and fill your spirit with joy. When will you choose to be happy? When will you begin to LIVE a life of happiness?

Reflections:

What is robbing me of my happiness?

Who has a hold of my happiness?

Why am I allowing others and outside factors to steal my happiness?

How long am I going to stay in this cycle?

When will I choose happiness?

LIVE

Your life to please God, not man.

L iving your life to please man will get you nowhere. You will constantly find yourself in a cycle of looking for affirmation and acceptance. Pleasing man, who is fickle, is dangerous and detrimental to your self-esteem, confidence and self-worth. When you think you have won someone over and they are pleased and excited for you, it can disappear in a matter of seconds depending on the person's mood or a bad decision you might make in the future. That is why you must live to please God. His approval is the thing that matters. Humans are flawed and emotional beings. When you seek another person's approval or acceptance you are not living for yourself, but for what that person thinks and feels towards you. Newsflash, you will never be able to please everyone, even on a good day someone will always be negative towards you. I learned this lesson in high school. A situation occurred in my home that put me at odds with my father. Growing up I wanted to please my parents and make them proud of me, but the summer of my senior year, I invited a friend over, knowing I was not supposed to have company when my parents were not there.

Well, lo and behold, my father came home and found this person there. Although nothing was going on, my dad blew up. He said things to me that hurt me to the core. He knew what type of person I was, but here he was speaking to me and calling me things that were not of my character. At that moment, I pledged to never seek my parents' approval of my life because no matter how hard I might try to do right, when I did do wrong, judgment and insults came that were not warranted. It took me a long time to reconcile my feelings, but I never again lived my life to make my father or anyone else proud of me. I decided that God and I were the only ones who mattered and when I fail, I only have God and myself to contend with. Today, I want you to make yourself a priority on your own terms. Stop looking for acceptance and approval from outside sources and lean on God. The only person who has the right to be disappointed in you, is you. We have a tendency to be our worse critics and knowing that is enough. It's time for you to make you the priority, hold yourself accountable and please no man, but God.

Reflections:

Who are you currently living to please or receive recognition from?

Why do you feel you need the approval of others?

What instances have you not met other's expectations, acceptance or approval? How did it make you feel?

When will you decide that the only acceptance you need is from God and yourself?

LIVE

Your life to be a "change agent" in someone's life.

What is a change agent? A change agent is someone who is a catalyst to helping someone become a better person. A change agent is someone who sees the potential in another and helps to pull it out of them. It is a person who speaks life into a person when they are down, stressed and emotionally depleted. A change agent is someone who assists in actions causing a person to change course for their betterment to reach their full potential. This is what we are called to do. We are not here to live a life solely focused on ourselves. Our mission in life is to help someone to be and do better. Change agents inspire, encourage, support, and evoke passion in others. Being a change agent is intentional and non-judgmental. It requires having a trusting relationship and effective communication. As a change agent, your duty is to make sure you highlight the best qualities in someone to encourage them to do their best, pursue a dream or change behaviors that are a hindrance to their success. Being a change agent does not require you to live or lead a "perfect" life. It only requires you to be a motivating factor to help direct a change in someone that would be beneficial to and for them. As a change agent, you must help others to see their value and hold them accountable for following through. You are simply helping to create a specific change. You are assisting them to see a different future than the one they see now. As a change agent, you speak life into a person's soul and spirit and reinvigorate a dead passion or dream that they have allowed to die or drop to the wayside. You are the cheerleader, the encourager and the mentor they need to make the transformation from a caterpillar to a butterfly. As a change agent, you must realize that you are not the center of attention, nor are you seeking recognition. You are simply doing for someone outside of yourself to reach their potential. I challenge you, be the change agent!

Reflections:

Who has been a change agent in your life?

How did they help you reach new potentials?

Who in your life can you act as a change agent for?

How will you assist them in reaching their potential?

Which men or women were used as change agents in the Bible? How did they affect someone's life or purpose? What can you learn from them?

LIVE

Your life according to God's agenda, not yours. You will find that God's agenda for your life is larger and far greater than what you have for yourself.

Jeremiah 29:11 says, "For I know the thoughts and plans that I have for you, says the Lord, thoughts and plans for welfare and peace and not for evil, to give you hope in your final outcome".

God is simply saying, "I've Got You!" You must keep in mind at all times that "Our Father Knows Best"! In all things, you must pray and seek God's direction. You must learn to consult with Him and meditate on the word before making decisions for your life. Is it wrong to plan? No, as I have stated before, you can plan anything you want, but one of the questions that must be asked is "is my plan God-led or Man-led?" In other words, are your plans being led by the spirit or the flesh? When your plans are spirit-led, it is for the greater good and the return is for God. You are not looking to serve yourself, but when it is flesh-led, you are only doing things that will give you immediate pleasure and gratification. You are looking to be lifted, pleased and the return is always for your benefit, not that of others. Secondly, you must realize that your plans can only go so far, because you are near-sighted, meaning you can only see what is before you because your vision is extremely limited. You cannot see what is to come, or what pitfalls might exist from taking the wrong path. When setting an agenda, *plan*, for your life you must pray that it is in God's will because you are here to serve Him and to fulfill the plan and purpose He has for your life. Remember, God's plan ensures your welfare, brings you peace and not strife, gives you hope and will always override any plan you have without consulting Him. Know this; you can never out do God!

Reflections:

What plans did you make in the flesh without consulting God?

Were those plans productive and yield the result you wanted?

What plans do you currently have in mind to pursue?

Will the plans place you in a position to help others?

Are the plans in alignment to God's plan for you?

LIVE

Stop making excuses and allowing FEAR to reside in your spirit. It is time for you to "seize the day"!

Fear! Fear is what keeps you in bondage. It is very easy to say, "I will not allow fear to take hold of me", but I know very well that it is not that easy. I began writing "Live, Learn, Grow", in 2011, but it took me until 2016, yes, five years later to complete it! I also started forming the groundwork for a non-profit organization during that same time and now five years later, I am feverishly working to bring it to life again. What happened in those five years ago? Fear happened. I allowed me to get in my head. I allowed excuses to take over and become the reason why I was not doing or pursuing. I allowed plans not coming together as "signs" that it was not the right time. I ALLOWED FEAR to dictate my moves. The bible says in 2 Timothy 1:7, "for God has not given us a spirit of fear, but of power and of love of a sound mind", and my mind at that time was full of noise. I was easily distracted, and I allowed myself to be distracted. Sometimes, you allow fear to take over because deep down you do not believe you are ready or you do not have what it takes to make things happen. You begin to self-sabotage and destroy the opportunities that come your way leaving you feeling guilty at times and unfilled. The longer you listen to the noise and dig yourself deeper into a rut, it becomes harder to overcome and destroy that sense of fear.

Pulling yourself out of fear's grasp is hard and takes a determined spirit to overcome the negative feelings and thoughts you have about yourself. I knew that I was not doing what I was supposed to do, but I rationalized and made excuses as to why I could not do it; and that is what we do; begin to rationalize why our sense of fear is right. We see others pursuing and doing and think "well good for them", but deep down have guilt because that success story could be our success, and there we have it, SUCCESS! As much as people want to be successful, that same amount is afraid of it and what it means for their future. You

18

have to come to a place of choosing to rest in fear and take the consequences or to come out of it, shut the noise out and rely on God to pull you through. When you are ready to face fear, you have to be ready to take risks, hear "no", run out of money, end relationships, open yourself up to trust, be disappointed and even hurt. You have to be willing to experience the pitfall before you can celebrate the wins in life. In the end, life is about choices and when you choose fear you shortchange yourself and miss out on opportunities for action, growth, maturity and success. What will you choose today; Fear or Success?

Reflections:

What are you afraid of pursuing?

Why are you afraid of allowing yourself to experience this new venture in life?

What experiences will you miss due to your fear?

What type of negative self-talk are you speaking that is holding you back?

Who can be an accountability partner for you?

Choose one of the things you are afraid of doing and begin to put it in action. Write down the moments you begin to become afraid and notate why?

What is the catalyst to your fear?

LIVE

You cannot wait for everything to be "perfect". In doing so, you will miss opportunities and blessings!

Nothing in life is and will never be perfect. Again, nothing in life will ever be perfect. It sets you up for the fall and disappointment, because you will forever be searching for the ideal thing. Can situations and circumstances come at the right time? Yes! Can you find someone with whom you have some much in common that the relationship is great? Yes. But, although those things can happen, it does not take much for them to go sour and that once then perfect moment, relationship, or job is now a thorn in your side. Society has set this culture of expectation that perfection can be reached and if you have not done so, then something is amiss with you. It makes you believe that fairy tales are real and there may be the "perfect" person for you. It makes you believe that you have to wait for the "perfect" circumstance, situation or place in life before you step out on faith to do or try anything. Perfect, in and of itself, is a state of opinion in belief. I say this because I can find a house that is right for me based on the design, space and surroundings, but to you would not be perfect. You cannot live your life waiting and hoping for conditions to be "perfect" or "right" for you to start doing. When you remove the boundaries of perfection, you start to live life the way it was meant to be lived. You will take more chances and seek new adventures. You will start that business or get into a relationship that will challenge you, but in the end, give you lessons and experiences you would have never learned or had. Perfection is an illusion at best. People want the perfect body, the perfect shape, the perfect children, the perfect husband, wife, career and the list can go on and on. But what happens when we do not live life due to seeking perfection? What happens when we wait for the perfect condition? When we wait, we take God out of the equation. We essentially tell God that we do not trust Him enough to give us what we need in every situation. We tell Him that He does not know what is true and right for us. Start living life to simply live! Start taking risks and seeking new adventures! Stop wasting your time due to waiting on the perfect time! It's time for you to simply live!

Reflections:

What opportunities have you missed by waiting on the perfect situation?

What is your ideal situation for you to start living?

Why do you believe things have to be perfect in order to be right?

What motto can you create to remind yourself to live life without the boundaries of perfectionism?

LIVE

To win one.

The statement "It's not about you" is very true. We live in an increasingly self-centered society where people are living in the mind frame of "it's all about me" and "what I can do for myself". People live a life chasing after one that only uplifts them never reaching back to help others. The gratification that they get is from the gains and accomplishments they have made, and it becomes like a drug; they have to push for more. But let us take a moment to think how much more gratifying life could be if I helped one, led one to Christ, showed one that there is a better way and lived life outside of myself to uplift, or encourage and motivate another person. I believe we get so wrapped up in our own life and problems that we forget that someone else needs uplifting as well. I am a firm believer that when you take your eyes off of your own problems and help someone else, our own problems do not seem so bad after all and we figure out a better way of handling it. I'm a professional school counselor and go to work daily to win a student back. I work in an urban, Title I school, and the neighborhood is not always forgiving. Working with this population is a struggle, but it is one worth the hard work and win! My students come from homes of single parents, being raised by grandparents, poverty and all types of abuse. Some of my students suffer from "hood life" mentality. What's that you ask?

The attitude of, "I have to be tough", being obstinate is being "hard", having an attitude or "I must be ready for whatever" no matter how silly it is, is the code of the hallways and school life. The students most affected by this are my young ladies. I am constantly speaking life into them trying to get them to understand that just because "you are from the hood, you don't have to be of the hood". I tell them where I grew up and how my neighborhood was and that if you want better and more for yourself you have to do better and leave the foolishness behind. The majority of what I say goes in one ear and out of the other, but I know they hear me and are just not ready to make the change; and although I would love to win them all, I settle for my one here, two there, and so on. I've been in this business for 18 years and won a lot and that gratification of seeing students want more and appreciate your encouragement is what I live for and it never disappoints. People need people. Winning one is not hard. There is nothing super special that is required of you. All that is required is that you place yourself in situations to set-up the win. You have to decide that helping someone is just as important as helping yourself. You have to decide that life is not always about you! We are not here to be alone in our walk. We are here to help pull others up. We are here to pray for one another. We are here to speak life into someone who is dying spiritually and mentally. We are here to help others reach a goal or desire. We are here to win! Who will you win?

Reflections:

Who "won" you and how did it change your life?

How did they help you?

Who have you "won"?

How were they affected?

How did it affect you?

If you have not "won" anyone to Christ, how can you open yourself to being alert to situations to win someone?

What walls do you need to knock down in order to "win" someone to Christ?

LIVE

*A life of pursuing your
purpose and passion.*

E very year I *live* for my birthday weekend. I start thinking and planning the activities months in advance by saving money, thinking of a theme, finding the perfect outfit, restaurants, new and fun places to go and sending out invitations giving people plenty of time to commit or decline before the MAIN event takes place. I search the internet for days trying to find the newest and best restaurants so that everyone can have a NEW experience with me. Sometimes I request a color scheme or for my guests to pay for activities (that are awesomely fun) instead of bringing a gift. Recently, I found out that not only do I look forward to my birthday, but some of my friends also look forward to seeing where it will be and what we will do. I mean it is a major weekend if I must say so, but it's just one event among many that takes place in my life. What if I took the passion and drive in life to live every day doing tasks to reach and pursue my blessings in life? What if I spent days, weeks, months planning and seeking God's instructions and directions to encounter the blessings He has for me, instead of thinking when and how can I achieve what I feel has been placed in me to do? What if I had devoted passionate time into encountering what God has for me, my life would be so much further along than where it is now. I would not be on this hamster wheel trying to catch up on the missed opportunities I have allowed to escape me.

We must remember that Jesus walked this earth fulfilling a purpose. He had a mission to show that He was the son of God and that "I Am" resided in Him. He healed people by moving and being in the presence of others, not planning the events and times of healing or ministering. Jesus lived! He woke daily with purpose on His heart and mind and lived a life of fulfilling his calling. In Mark 5, we see that Jesus made several encounters. He healed a man possessed with evil spirits, a little girl who was on her deathbed and a woman with an issue of blood, (and she was healed because she was pursuing a healing), and the encounters were not only an encounter for those involved, but changed lives of those connected to each person. That was His purpose in performing those healings and miracles. In the grand scheme of life, we have been blessed with everything we will ever be blessed with, but it is up to us to live a life of pursuing those blessings. We are not here to just exist; we are here to walk in purpose that will give life meaning, definition and character. It is up to us to do the work and put as much into it as we do when we plan for frivolous things that do not matter in the big picture of life. When we spend time getting our soul and spirit connected to hear from the Holy Spirit to begin pursuing, we not only fulfill our calling and purpose, but we become blessings to others and that is what this life is all about. It is time to put effort into walking in our purpose just as we plan major events in our life. It is time to tap into our gifts and talents and use them to birth what God has placed in us to do! It is high time to start pursuing and claiming what is yours!

Reflections:

What are your passions?

How can your passion be turned into purpose?

Do you know your purpose? If you do not know your purpose pray and meditate on God's word to enlighten you.

What is preventing you from living a life of pursuing your purpose?

How can you change your thought process to begin living a life of pursuing your passion and purpose?

What is a hindrance that you need to give up right now to start living?

LIVE

To be a testimony.

We all have tests and trials. We all go through things in which we learn lessons from. But what do we do with those lessons? Do we keep them to ourselves or share them with others? I have suffered for years with gastrointestinal problems. I have spent nights and days balled up in a fetal position unable to move or breathe. I have spent countless nights crying out to God to help and heal me. I went from doctor to doctor and none could tell me specifically what was wrong with my digestive system. I took tests upon tests that always yielded the same results. Trying to figure out what was wrong was a daunting and exhausting experience. I have had doctors to tell it my pain or experience was all in my head. I have had doctors to call me a hypochondriac looking for attention. I changed my eating habits to reduce the pain and episodes. I *tried* to do everything I could think of to get better, but there was no success. My stomach issues tested my faith and belief in healing, but as I grew in understanding and my faith walk, I began to get stronger and my belief in my healing grew. I remember waking up one morning hearing instructions about what to read and do. I immediately got out of bed and read 2 Kings 5:14 where the prophet Elisha sent instructions to King Naaman to dip himself 7 times in the Jordan to be healed of his leprosy. I read the scriptures aloud, took my oil and anointed my body as instructed 7 times, and as I drove to work every day for 7 days I spoke healing to my body in detail.

I cannot say the day or moment I stopped having issues, all I can remember is one day being prompted by the spirit as I listened to a song about healing that it dawned on me that I had not had any pain, episodes or nights of crying in months. My healing was not immediate, and it was not without growing in faith. It took 20 years for my healing to manifest in the present. It took 20 years for me to grow and mature in my walk and trust God with my all.

It took 20 years to know that God is my healer and that He will sustain me to accomplish the purpose He has for me. I praise God for my mother who would come over and find me in a ball on the floor, get me to my bed and stay with me until the pain subsided. I praise God for the relationship I had and how God blessed me with a man that helped me and was there mentally, physically and emotionally. I praise God for the hurt, pain and time I spent in despair calling out for Him. I praise God for being there in my darkest hours of need, but I praise God because I have a testimony, one of many to share with someone who is sick, in pain, in despair ready to give up and give in. I praise God because He is Jehovah Rapha! He is the Lord who heals you! And although I know I will face other challenges, tests and trials I know without a doubt that I will be an overcomer. Why, because my testimony from the past will carry me through! Remember, your testimony is not JUST for you, it is for the uplifting and encouraging of the body of Christ.

Reflections:

What is your testimony?

How has your testimony grown you?

Who have you helped with your testimony?

If you have not helped anyone with your testimony, how can you use your testimony to help someone now?

Have you been blessed by someone's testimony? How did it affect you?

LIVE

Life being a blessing to others through actions, speech, giving or deeds.

Blessing someone is so easy, yet many of us have a hard time doing it because we tend to make it conditional. We make it conditional dependent upon our emotions and that is not being pure of heart. I always ask people, what if God decided not to bless you because of His "feelings" toward you. Where would you be today? And with that comes a very long stare and pause. Right, God does not hold conditions over us, nor do emotional feelings come into play. He does not make His blessings dependent on our actions, because if He did that we would never wake up! Some people get caught up in the nuisances of what a blessing is, how large it has to be or how much do I have to give. The word says in 2 Corinthians 9: 7, that God loves a cheerful giver, one who gives from the heart, one who is not reluctant, but willing. Romans 15:1-3, says that we are to help our neighbor and not simply live to do things that please ourselves. In essence we are here to bless and help others in need. We are here to uplift and encourage. We are here to help someone who is down financially, emotionally, spiritually and mentally. We are here to help bear one another's trials in times of despair. We are here to give so that others may have. We must remember that the small things in life matter. A simple hello and a genuine "how are you doing?" in which you stay to hear the person's response, can truly bless a person and goes a long way.

Just as we are here to be a testimony, we are here to be blessings as well. One year for teacher's appreciation week I decided to give hand-written notes to every teacher I worked with on my grade level as well as school staff. I took time to think about what each person contributed and how their contribution affected our students. The response I received from the staff was one of shock, appreciation and thanks. They could not believe I had written individual notes for each person (I'm guessing they asked each other) because throughout the day I received many "thank you's, "I can't believe you wrote all of us individual notes" and "you don't know how much your words mean". Did it take time? Yes. Did I want to do it from the heart? Yes. You see, I saw a need. I saw that people were stressed. I saw that people were ready to give up. I saw what was needed because I needed it as well. When we bless others, we have to pay attention to their needs. We have to watch, listen and respond at the right time, when it is least expected and without announcing when and what you are going to do. You just do it! When we bless others, we receive a blessing in return. Blessings are unexpected prayers answered at the right time without notice. Your blessing does not have to be monumental; it just needs to be from the heart, intentional and on purpose.

Reflections:

What is your idea of a "blessing"?

Have you been blessed by someone in a time of need? How did it make you feel?

How did you bless someone in a time of need?

If you have not blessed someone in what ways can you begin to help others?

LIVE

A life set apart from the world.

As a toddler, my family lived in an apartment complex in Pleasant Grove outside of Dallas, TX that was not too far from where my dad was going to college at the time. I remember the kids always picking on me and how I would try to fit in, but never seemed able to do so. Now, fast forward to my elementary years when we moved to Oak Cliff, a "better" area so to speak than where I spent my toddler years, but I didn't escape the bullying. My elementary school years consisted of me proving my toughness, standing up for my friends and using my intellect to win others over by always having the answer "to gain some school street cred", but by 5th and 6th grade I was still labeled "stuck up" and "Miss she's too good for us". In the 6th grade the "bullying" got worse, because the mean girls had made it their mission to make my life miserable. I remember running home from school one day crying my eyes out. My feelings were so hurt, and my self-esteem was in the pits. My mother was at home that day and she said something to me that changed my life from that moment on. She told me that the kids at the school did not know the REAL me and that I was a bright, funny and beautiful girl. She said I should not let people's words and actions toward me defeat my spirit and to continue being me whether they liked me or not because in the end they were missing out.

That talk gave me the courage to face the next day and I was never the same. However, things never got better I just knew how to respect myself, maintain my self-esteem and handle the bullies with the smart mouth I developed as a defense mechanism. Once I entered middle and high school, I did not care what anyone said, but I always wondered why I was not like everyone else. I wanted to "fit in" with the crowd and not be so obviously "NOT" of the crowd, but it just was not in me. I often would wonder why I was not "hood" enough, "real" enough, "sister-girl" enough. It was not until my early 30's that it hit home for me. I had grown in my spiritual and faith walk, learned more about being who I was called to be and began to take stock of my life. I was a small group leader working with young ladies and as a school counselor; I made it my mission to pour into my girls at school. I spent a lot of my days counseling my girls to be who they are no matter what and to stand out from the rest, because they are special.

Finally, it hit me like a ton of bricks one Sunday after church while I was speaking with my dad, "Different Ain't Bad". You see being different, *set apart,* is what we are called to be. Our existence on this Earth is not to be and do like other people, instead we are placed here with a call on our life, a purpose and what that looks like for me does not look the same for someone else. Being set apart is walking your own path. It is being comfortable in your own skin and having that "something" people cannot quite put their finger on. Our life's story should not be one that the world is familiar with just because we have to coexist in it. We were made to stand out and when you walk in your greatness, your uniqueness, people will recognize and respect you for that. They will know that your spirit is different and change the way they interact with you. When you tap in to your spirit man and live in sync with it you will be able to love you in your entirety. My challenge for you is to be *SET APART* and be of the spirit and not of the flesh seeking to appease the masses. It's time to be different! It's time to live the *SET APART* life!

Reflections:

If you are SET APART, how do you maintain the balance between being in the world and not of the world?

How are you treated in relation to respect?

Do you find people treat you "of the world" or do they give you "special" treatment? What does that look like?

If you are following the world, how can you start living from the inside out?

Are you investigative and inquiring of others (meaning do you accept what you see and go along with worldly views) - If you answered yes, what does it look like? If you answered no, what steps can you take to begin to be inquiring of others' spirit-man?

LIVE

A life of encounters, not events.

Encounter: to meet (someone) without expecting or intending to; to come face-to-face; to come upon or experience especially unexpectedly. *Merriam-Webster's Learner's Dictionary*

The words I want to highlight in discussing living a life of encounters are *meet, experience*, and *unexpectedly*. Day to day we usually live by events. We get excited about parties, birthdays, weddings, births, planned activities, milestones, job interviews, you name it. We put thought into planning events and in making contingency plans in case the event does not go as planned. We think about those involved and how to make the event a wonderful experience. Most events are superficial, meaning we do not spend time digging deeper into the connections that will be made upon those in attendance. I am a great party planner, or so I believe. I mean I think about every detail and how others will perceive and enjoy it. I want my parties to not only be fun for me, but leave a lasting impression on those who attend. I buy gifts and give-a-ways, find out what people's interests are and try to incorporate those for an experience of a lifetime. But once that event is over, it's over. My guests have had a wonderful experience and always leave with smiles on their faces, but I may or may not see the attendee until the next year or never and it will become a moment in time experience.

One Sunday morning sermon, Dr. Leroy Thompson, was teaching about awakening the force of the soul, he said something that caught my attention, "Jesus Christ was an encounter, not an event" and "no more living a life of events, but life with God is a life of encounters." WOW! That was illuminating to me. It spoke volumes and I immediately wrote, "live a life of encounters, not events, meaning, stop living moment to moment, but live a life of "doing for others" and "pursuing what is already yours." This is where those three words come into play: *meet, experience* and *unexpectedly*. Each day we wake is indeed a blessing and an opportunity to be a blessing to someone in return. We constantly *meet* people in passing and generally give them a slight smile and a dry "how are you", in which we really do not want them to tell us how they are doing. The majority of us never step out intentionally to make each *unexpected* meeting with a person an *experience* that will change their thought process or course of action. We live in a society in which going deeper with a stranger could be seen and viewed as weird, but how many times has someone asked you "how are you" and you just wanted to purge.

How many times have you had the unexpected opportunity to speak a word of encouragement to someone in need? How many times have you intentionally listened to what was not said and answered with what the person needed? An encounter is meant to change a person for the better. It is meant to be an experience that one will never forget. As a school counselor, I always meet with students unexpectedly due to individual counseling, teacher referrals, parent consultation or a crisis. In each meeting, I try to speak words of encouragement, guidance and understanding into their spirits that will make a lasting impression, something they can remember and hold on to. I purposely turn the events or situations into an encounter, because by turning it into an encounter a person's disposition changes and becomes more open. This is the same as what happens when we have an encounter with the Holy Spirit. It is unexpected, leaves an impression and changes us for the better. Jesus was the encounter. Each day that He walked this Earth, He spoke into someone's life and changed it for the better. He left an impression upon those who walked with Him who were able to become walking encounters. He did not do it for the moment in time or for fame and recognition. He did it to be a blessing, to uplift and to encourage. You too are a walking encounter! The Holy Spirit resides in you, and you have the ability to speak into someone's life and bless them. You are qualified to turn events into encounters!

Reflections:

How do you live your life? Are you living for self for living to give back to others?

What can you do to make each opportunity an encounter and not just an event?

Who have you had an encounter with in which they or their situation was changed for the better?

1. What did they say or do?
2. How did you grow from it?

Reflect on a time in which you made an encounter. Describe the encounter and how you felt afterwards.

How can you turn events into encounters?

LIVE

To be an Ananias (giver of grace).

W hat is "grace"?

Grace: unmerited divine assistance give[n] [to] humans for their regeneration or sanctification. A virtue coming from God. Favor. A special favor. Disposition to or an act or instance of kindness, courtesy or clemency. The quality or state of being considerate or thoughtful. *Merriam-Webster's Learner's Dictionary*

Grace! If not for God's grace where would we all be! We are not perfect beings, albeit, some of us strive to be, it is never obtained, because we can, nor will ever be perfect no matter how hard we try. That is why we have God's grace. Grace is not conditional. It is not choosy or temperamental. It does not hold grudges or take account of wrongs. It is simple favor! God's unmerited favor and the love He has for you. We are quick to put someone in the "dog house" because of what they have done, but what if God did us that way. We are quick to dismiss a person due to their past or background. But what if God held that over our heads? We are quick to deny assistance to people because we feel they can do better if they tried a little harder. What is God put us in that situation? In the bible is a story of a man named Ananias. Ananias was a discipline who lived in Damascus. The Lord came to him in a vision and told him to go meet Saul because he, Ananias, would be the one to lay hands on Saul's eyes restoring his vision, but there was a huge problem that rested in Ananias's spirit.

The problem was Saul's past gave way to doubt and hesitation and Ananias was not trying to have that. Saul was a persecutor of those who believed in Jesus. He threatened, beat and murdered those who proclaimed to be followers of Christ. Therefore, Saul was someone to not trust and be afraid of. And with that type of history, Ananias was not inclined to want to go and "assist" Saul. He had doubt. He was clearly hesitant. But when God leads and tells you to do something, no matter how much you do not want to, you do it! Ananias gave all kinds of excuses, but he had a purpose and his purpose was greater than his fear. We must understand that sometimes being used by God will not be the popular thing to do. It may not even make sense, but that is what happens when God gives us grace. In today's time, there are a lot of Thomas's out there. We doubt, hesitate and hold back from helping someone due to their past. But what we do not understand is that when we help and show someone favor, in spite of their background we are the catalyst and sower, and God will reap the harvest.

We have to be like Ananias and give of ourselves to do what God tells us to do. We must never underestimate how our kindness, favor, forgiveness and our grace will impact and help others. We are all just one day of grace away from not being here due to some unforeseen incident, but God bestows upon us His grace daily without us asking for it. We must learn that it is not our right to be the judge over who will receive grace from us. We must learn to not hold back, but instead heed the word, use our discernment and be givers of grace. We must learn to trust God and allow him to lead us in all situations and decisions when we are faced to extend grace. Ananias went and completed the task given him. He allowed himself to be used and did as instructed. In so doing, Saul was given a new lease on life. His eyes were opened and for the first time he saw the true light, the truth and his life transformed from that day forward; and Paul was birthed. How powerful is that? How powerful is it to be used to lead someone to be the greater form of their former self? How powerful is it to win someone to Christ by extending grace? In the current state that we live in, grace is needed. We need each other more than ever now and what we need is grace. It is time to be givers of grace. Are you ready?

Reflections:

Have you been in a situation in which someone extended grace to you? If so, describe the situation and highlight the transformation that took place with you in response to this action.

How has God extended His grace towards you?

When was the last time you recognized God's grace in your life?

What does extending grace to someone look like for you?

What would be an obstacle to you extending grace to someone?

LIVE

A life trusting God.

At the beginning of 2008 I decided that I was ready to get my finances together to purchase a home. I had set in my mind that this was going to be a worthwhile process and I was in for the long haul. I began paying off my debt, God led me to the right apartment complex that was perfect for my budget and things were set in motion. Now along the 4 years that it took for me to prepare to move, I had some trials and tribulations. This apartment was my place of Marah. It was a turning point and dry place for me. BUT GOD! I came out of that apartment and found a house in a neighborhood I had my eye on for 2 years. Fast forward to 2012, I move in, get money back that I put down and things are fantastic. Then it happened. A year in, my payments went up so much that I did not think I would be able to stay. I almost panicked, but I had to remember how I got this house and what I did before I moved into my home. You see, I prayed, sowed seed, and believed for this house. I anointed my house with scriptures and gave my home back to God before the sheetrock was put in. This was not my house, but God's. So, I prayed and asked for direction and did as the Holy Spirit directed. I called and got my payment reduced to an affordable amount and 2 years later the payments were back down to being manageable. Living a life trusting God is to trust Him with all things our human capacity cannot see, because we can only see what is immediately before us. Trusting God is having a firm reliance on His ability and in his character to do what He says and believe in His promises. Trusting God is placing your trust and faith in Him to work situations and circumstances out and not get in the way. We must learn to place ourselves in His custody and know that HE will always provide. Trusting God is staying committed to Him daily and relying on Him to get us through when we cannot possibly see any way out. Trusting God is believing that He will! We must believe that

He is our provider, stronghold, deliverer, director and protector. Living a life trusting God is knowing that He will never fail you! Remember "a man's mind plans his way, but the Lord directs his steps and makes them sure"-Proverbs 15:9

Reflection:

Are you trusting God? If so how? In what area(s) of our life? If you are not trusting God, what situation has God brought you out of that you saw no possible way out of?

What are you believing God for at this time in your life?

How has your faith waivered in trusting God?

Have you given up control and placed yourself in His care for all of your needs? If so, how? If you have not, how can you start to?

LIVE
In the YES!

A re you an optimistic or pessimistic person? Do you see the positive side of everything or are you the person who is the naysayer? Living in the YES is living in the promises of God. Living in the YES is knowing that there are no "NO's" when God makes a promise, and a denial or delay does not mean God is not going to bless you with what you need. Living in the YES is living in a positive state of mind knowing that God is in control of your promotion, increase, healing, deliverance, or whatever you need. Know that God functions in victory and living in victory is living in the YES! We must be careful as to what we pray and ask God for. A lot of times we want things that are outside of God's will and when we get them we believe it to be our "YES", when in fact it is our "NO". Living in the will of God is living in the YES. It is being connected to Him building a sincere and committed relationship. It is desiring the things of the Lord and not of the flesh. It is questioning those things of the world and using our wisdom and discernment to guide us to make the best decisions. It is staying in tune and connected to the Holy Spirit and trusting God! Living in the YES is saying YES to God when our flesh wants us to run for the hills. In my late 20's, I rejoined Oak Cliff Bible Fellowship as an adult. I became involved in the Single's Ministry and was all in! I mean the ministry took over my life! I found a small group and fell in love with the young women.

We were all looking to grow in the word and build genuine relationships. After about a year into the group, our fearless leader told us she would be stepping down and suggested that I take over the group. My immediate reaction was, "not me!" but she saw something in me that I did not see. She was my change agent! I struggled with this decision. I mean I was in a state of NO! I was telling God that I was not ready to lead these young women to grow in the word and be strong women of God. I did not feel

I was in a place of honor to lead, but what I came to realize was that it was not just about me. It was about what God would do to and through me. I wrestled with the decision for about two weeks before I told her I would take over and when I said YES, I felt as if God had been preparing me in my struggle. He had set things in motion and given me the tools I would need to grow and move us in the right direction. I was definitely prepared. It came naturally to me. It was not this hard and arduous task. It was a beautiful and fun experience each and every time I met with those young ladies. It was not about me saying YES to the group, but it was about me saying YES to God for my relationship to grow with Him. See, living in the YES is yielding to God and allowing Him in to do a work in you to bring you closer to Him. Are you ready to live in the YES?

Reflection:

What has God placed on your heart to do?

In order to say YES, what must you give up?

Will living in the YES be hard for you? If so, how?

What decision have you been struggling with that is keeping you from living in the YES?

Do you feel you are prepared to say and live in the YES? If yes, describe how. If no, explain why not.

LIVE

The life God has ordained for you
to have with NO apologies!

Are you living your life to the fullest, or are you living in your own shadow afraid to step out to be who you were born to be? A lot of us never live to our full potential because we are more concerned with what other people think or say. Our society has labeled people who march to their own drum, eccentric, but those people are living a full life with no apologies. Albeit, some of the things they do may not seem "kosher" to you, these individuals are happy doing their own thing and do not care what others think. The key is not caring "what others think". We are caught up in placing our worth and acceptance into man's hands, neglecting the one who matters the most. We look to man for approval from the way we dress, cars we drive, where we live, schools our kids attend to the types of clothing we wear, stores we shop, even down to what we eat! Newsflash, man did not write your story! Man, did not ordain you before you were to be! Man, has no say over your life! We have to stop looking to man to dictate how we "should" or "should not" live. We have to start tapping into what God wants from us, and how we feel about ourselves and live life out loud! We have to stop judging ourselves. Yes, we judge ourselves! We are our worst critics. Have you ever noticed people who do not care about what people have to say? We generally do not find these individuals stressed, depressed, angry or bitter; they are usually even kill types who go with the flow and find laughter and enjoyment in what they do. The expectations of the "world" do not bog them down. They have usually found their passion and purpose, flow in it and accept who they are, where they are and where they might go. On the flipside, we have people who make a sizeable amount of money a year and people who, for a lack of a better word, "hate" on them because of that; or we scrutinize those who live with just the necessities. No matter where you are in life, what you are doing, where you are trying to go, do it for God and do what makes you happy! Stop apologizing for a life that God has blessed you to have. Stop apologizing for following your heart and passion! Stop apologizing for doing YOU! It is time to focus on what matters the most, your happiness. Get ready, set, GO... live your life OUT LOUD!

Reflections:

Everyone has a drive to do or be something more, what do you always see yourself doing?

Why have you not made the move to make it happen?

Make a list of your hindrances and write how you are going to overcome them.

What are the pros and cons to living your life OUT LOUD, doing what you were created to do?

LIVE
A life of positive influence.

What is a role model? Per Merriam-Webster's dictionary, a role model is someone who another person admires and tries to be like; a person whose behavior in a particular role is imitated by others. Basically, a person you would like to be like due to the things you have seen them do or accomplishments they have made. Most role models are people in the public eye. We haphazardly place this term on entertainers, actors, athletes, and others without really considering if those individuals are "worthy" of the title. We try to force these individuals to be role models making positive impacts on our younger generation, but is that fair to them. A lot of those individuals follow their dreams, passions and make it, which is a great story, but they do not necessarily live a life worthy of following or imitating. I truly believe we must be careful placing titles on people. We must teach our children that role models leave positive impressions and ignite a passion in others that cause them to pursue their dreams. Living a life of positive influence in today's time is so crucial. I believe that we are all placed here to influence others and we can do it two ways, positively or negatively. I am not saying we must be perfect in our walk, because in truth, no one is and will ever be perfect. But what I am saying is that we have to be intentional in leading others down a positive road in their daily walk. We are always being watched and someone is always checking for you. They are watching what you do and say. They are forever lining up your actions and deeds to make sure you are being real and honest.

Today, it is so easy to monitor people due to social media and the internet. These two vehicles have allowed us to follow people and give our input to their lives and it give us a false sense of connection, therefore it is crucial to monitor what we do and say. As an educator, I strive to set an example for the students I work with, as well as in my personal life, I strive to set an example of pursuing a life of positivity. Living a life of positive influence is living in your truth. It is knowing your pitfalls and knowing how to overcome them. It is being transparent admitting your mistakes and working through them. It is watching what you do and say as to not cause others to "fall". It is knowing that you are a work in progress, but allowing others to see your growth. It is striving to make the best decisions and not follow your flesh to corruption and deceit. It is allowing the spirit to work through you to reach others. It is empowering, motivating and inspiring others to be their BEST selves. It is speaking life into others and showing them there is a better way. It is choosing optimism! I challenge you to give it a try! I challenge you to begin making positive deposits into people's spirits! It's time for you to be a positive influencer!

Reflections:

Who was or is your role model? Why?

Do you consider yourself a positive influencer? Why? Why not?

How can you live a life of optimism, positivity?

Have you helped someone lead a life of positivity? If so, how?

What do you need to change in your daily walk to begin living a life as a positive influencer?

Has anyone ever told you that you were a role model or that you inspire them? If yes, what did they say and how did it make you feel? If no, what steps can you take to be a positive inspiration for someone?

~Prayer~

Dear Heavenly Father, I come to you asking that you show me how to LIVE for you! Lord show me how to live the life you created me for and use me to help others the way you see fit. Lord, guide me in living life on purpose daily touching those you lead me to. Lord teach me how to live for you honoring the gifts, talents, and purpose you have placed within me. Father, I thank you for the life you blessed me to have and ask that you show me how to encourage others to live the life they were meant to live. Lord help me to live in the now pursuing all that you have for me. Teach me to be content in the now! Lord prepare me that I may be a giver of grace, forgiving and loving people where they are. Lord help me to live encounter to encounter and not event to event. Father, help me to not live in the shadows of fear. Help me to be strong resting my assurance in your power. Lord bless my journey, ordering my steps, leading me to my future. Help me to stay connected to you surrounding myself with those who have a heart for you and desire to lead a life fulfilling our plan. Thank you for your direction, mercy, grace, and love. Thank you for loving me where I am and preparing me for my future. I pray that I will continue to honor you in my daily walk and pray that when I fall, I can rely on my faith and trust in you to steer me back home. Father thank you being omniscient, omnipresent, and faithful! I will bless your name and give you praise for in the cross is my deliverance, redemption, and victory! Amen!

~Affirmation~

I will live my life according to the plan and purpose for which I was created. I will not allow fear to hold me hostage and steal my future. I will live to bless others and help them to live the life they are meant to live. I will speak life into those who are hurting, lost, depressed and have allowed life to conquer them. I will lift others up, proclaiming victory for their lives! I am blessed! I am a conqueror! I am a giver of grace! I am a role model! I am a positive light! I am victory! I am free! I am a peacemaker! I have all the power in me to be great and I will walk in my greatness! I will no longer allow my thoughts and past to defeat me! I am a new creature in Christ and I will live life on purpose and with purpose! I will seek opportunities to win one! I will invest time in loving myself growing from my pain and past! I will no longer seek man's approval for my life! I will live in truth and respect myself at all times! I choose happiness and will not allow negative thoughts to consume me! I will LIVE life with NO apologies! I choose to LIVE and I will start LIVING today!

Now that we have walked through ways of how to start living, it is now time to learn from life's lessons. Many of us walk through life never learning from our mistakes, relationships, trials, upsets or disappointments. We hold on to the hurts and stay on an emotional rollercoaster complaining and having pity parties. We become bitter and angry developing pessimistic attitudes. We start to live in dysfunction and become consumed with negative thoughts. It is time to say no more and learn how to press your way and move on from the pain and disappoint. It is time to LEARN!

"When life gives you a basket of rotten apples, dump them out and pick fresh ones." –Dedra Colston

Are you ready to LEARN?

LEARN

When to LET GO! It will save
you a lot of stress, heartaches,
disappointments, trials, and TIME!

I am the first to say letting go is h. a. r. d. It is a very real struggle, especially when you have your heart tied to it. Whether it is a job, relationship, family member or issue, letting go requires growth and a mind determined to do so. The hardest thing I have had to do was to let go of someone I was in love with. I had other relationships and thought I was "in love", but it was not until I was in my early 20's that I discovered what love was. I had never met someone with whom I was willing to pour into and allow to see the real me, inside and out. We dated for a few years and then there was the dreaded "break up". We were young and probably needed to break up, but what we did not do was move on. We continued to revisit a pseudo-relationship which was detrimental to me because although I knew he did not want me the same way anymore, I continued to bask in the comfort of our familiarity with one another. This pseudo-relationship went on for a few years after the break up, and although I dated other people and lived life, I always held on to this notion that "he" was the "one" for me. Years passed, relationships went nowhere, and I had to come to terms with the fact that I was causing my lack in progress in my love life. I was holding out hoping that this person would eventually want me like they used to, that this person would finally see that I was the one for him. But that never happened, and I knew that it was not going to.

There were signs and many conversations, but it was not until I told God and myself that I was ready for more and ready for who He predestined for me to be with. See, in order to get our blessings, in order to heal, in order to move forward in life, we have to let go of what is holding us back. Sometimes we are our own worst enemy. I should know, I was mine. I was limiting my opportunities of meeting the person I could have possibly married. I was hindering my progress. I was diminishing my chances of meeting the ONE for me, and when I finally listened and LET GO, I was FREE. Did it hurt? YES! But, I have yet to regret the decision. If your parent, friend or significant other has hurt or disappointed you and you are still holding on, it is time to LET GO! If you are still holding on to a mistake that you made that changed the trajectory of your life, it is time to learn from it and LET it GO! If your job passed you over for a well-deserved promotion and you are still upset about it, it is time to LET it GO! Disney got one thing right when they made Frozen, the song, "Let it Go"! That songs speaks volumes. LET GO! It is time to be free from what has held you hostage for years! Are you ready?

Reflections:

What situation(s) have you allowed to hold you hostage? Why?

If your situation has caused you to become bitter, depressed, or pessimistic, why are you still holding on?

Why is it hard for you to let go?

What will it take for you to let go? (not dependent on the other person(s))?

What steps will you take?

How will letting go change your life?

LEARN

To praise God through the tough times, sad moments and hurt. Know that your faith and character are being tested and molded!

The year was 2013, my third year as a Professional School Counselor in middle school. I had spent the first two years getting my feet wet trying to figure out my place and learn as much as I could about the school culture and teachers. I had been an elementary school counselor for 7 years and this was very different and trying. I was beginning to feel as if I was getting the hang of middle school and the students when a "new" job role was placed in my lap, testing coordinator. Now, I was trying to figure out how I was supposed to meet the needs of the students socially, emotionally, and academically, as well as prepare and coordinate local and state testing at the same time. Well, let me just say, I hated my job! I wrote an entire blog about it, cried almost every day on my drive to work, screamed to the top of my lungs once I got home, cried some more, and eventually ended up in the hospital. I was stressed and depressed. I felt ineffective as a counselor because I was no longer focused on meeting the needs of the students and staff, but was more focused on preparing for test after test after test. I was working 16-18 hours a day, including working at least 8 hours on the weekends. My life was consumed with doing something that was not connected to the reason I paid to get a Master's degree. I was becoming angry and bitter. I was mean and not easy to approach. I literally wanted to quit my job with no future job in sight. I had reached a point of no return. I was ready to walk away from it all. Then the Holy Spirit step in.

One Sunday, I did not go to church due to having to prep for an upcoming test, so I decided to have my own bible study. I am a believer that everything works out the way it is supposed to, even when we must go through the valley to get to the mountaintop. Well, as God would have it, I was led to a scripture during my prayer time. I had no idea what I was going to study, but God did. After praying I opened my bible up to Colossians 2:23-24 which says "whatever may be your task, work at it heartily (from the soul), as [something done] for the Lord and not for men, 24 Knowing [with all certainty] that it is from the Lord [and not from men] that you will receive the inheritance which is your [real] reward. [The One Whom] you are actually serving [is] the Lord Christ (the Messiah)"- The Amplified Bible. That verse changed my life from that moment forward. I went into praise mode, crying, and thanking God for hearing my cry! I changed my outlook and performed my new job with a new attitude. I also continued to pray that God would remove that task from my job duties. I reached out to earthly powers to be and voiced my concerns and experiences due to the new job duty.

You see, when you decide to trust God, and put your focus on Him and Him alone, the gates of heaven will open for you and from it will your blessings flow. In a matter of a couple of months, that job duty, as well as few others, were taken away from counselors and we were to solely focus on what our NEW job description outlined, which had everything to do with why I earned a Master's degree. Can you say this was a "hallelujah moment"! I do not know what your thorn is. I do not know what you are going through, but what I do know is that when you turn it over to God and allow Him to be the master of the situation, you learn how to grow in faith and depend on Him and not yourself to handle a situation. My year of hating my job turned into a year of learning that in all I do, make sure to do it for the Lord and trust Him to deliver me from any depths I might find myself in. The year gave me a new outlook, toughen me and I learned to not stress about things outside of my control anymore. It developed and moved my faith to a new level and allowed me to help others in a similar situation. It is time to get your praise on and allow the ONE above to handle it for you!

Reflections:

What are you struggling with or going through right now?

Do you believe that praising God in the midst will deliver you from your situation? Why or Why not?

Are you willing to give your situation over to God? Why or Why not?

Has there ever been a time when you thought you could not make it through? If so, what was it and how did you overcome it?

What have you learned about yourself from your current situation?

LEARN

People are toxic. You must remove yourself before their toxic ways begin to set disbelief, doubt, stress, anger, disappointment, low self-esteem, and defeat in your life.

Definition of Toxic:

Tox•ic [tóksik] adjective

1. involving something poisonous; relating to or containing a poison or toxin.
2. Deadly; causing serious harm or death

Noun

tox•ics plural

1. Poisonous substance; a poison or toxin.

In the late 2000's, Britney Spears had a song titled "Toxic" on her fourth album, "In the Zone", in which she sings about being addicted to a lover that is obviously not good for her, but she wants the person even though the relationship is dangerous and unhealthy. How many of us are like this? How many are drawn to unhealthy relationships? How many of us decide to stay in a relationship that is killing us emotionally, mentally, and spiritually? Well, newsflash… you are now a TOXIC person. You have been corrupted and need to be set free. We are all guilty of staying past our expiration date. We know good and well when a person is not right for us, but for some reason we have it set in our minds that we can DEAL! Sometimes we are even blind to the notion that a person or a relationship is not right for us because we cannot or will not recognize it for our own selfish reasons. Well how can you tell if a person or relationship is TOXIC? Let us start with the basics; a toxic person is anyone! It could be a family member, friend, coworker, spouse, church member, neighbor, or boss you name it. What makes them toxic are these following characteristics:

1) Manipulate you or a situation
2) Complain
3) Controlling
4) Self-centered
5) Uncompromising
6) Feeds off negativity
7) Never uplifting or encouraging
8) Possessive nature
9) Inconsiderate
10) Liar
11) Disrespectful
12) User
13) Plays on your emotions
14) Needy
15) Negative
16) Mental, emotional, physical, and verbal abuser

These characteristics do not happen at one time. A person may exhibit one of these and that one is enough to destroy you. However, there are some people who possess a combination of these characteristics and if so, they are most definitely TOXIC with a big flashing sign above their head saying, *"WARNING! DANGER! ENTER AT YOUR OWN RISK!"* and without fail, someone will choose to do so or will choose to stay because they have been drained of life! You see what happens is that there is "something" about this person or relationship that keeps one hanging around. If it is family, that "something" will be obligation or guilt. If it is a romantic relationship, it is the person's charisma or the memories and love you feel for them; or it is your need to help or fix that person which will never happen. What happens instead is their poisonous ways begin to infiltrate your mind and spirit leading you to doubt your own sense of what is right and wrong. It begins to erode and corrupt your sense of being causing you to doubt yourself, lowering your self-esteem, confidence and increasing a dependency on them. Toxic people are dangerous! They are not for me, nor you! They are here to kill, steal and destroy your spirit and that is NOT what God wants for our relationships with others to look like.

Toxic people do not know any other way to function and would deny that they even possess any of these characteristics. Even if you pointed them out, they might attempt to improve if they truly care for you, but 9 times out of 10 it is to no avail. Over the years, I have learned to distance myself from toxic people, but every once in a while, my helping spirit attaches to one and really tries help them be a better person. Well, I have learned in my helping, that everyone does not want help. They may see nothing wrong with the way they are and enjoy resting in their corrupt ways, because on the far-left end of the spectrum are those that "FEED" into their behavior, or they too, are surrounded by other toxic people. It is time to evaluate your circle. It is time to let go of those who bring your spirit down when they are in your presence. Let go of people who are spiteful and mean-spirited. Let go of people who are controlling and manipulative. Let go of people who want to tear you down with words.

Let go of people who do not show you that they have your BEST interests in mind and are inconsiderate of your feelings. Healthy relationships consist of being encouraging, supportive, considerate, loving, respectful, honest, accepting, enduring and shows unconditional positive regard and love towards another. Healthy relationships are not one-sided, but are mutual. Healthy relationships are not demanding, but always communicate with love. Most importantly healthy relationships are forgiving and maintain realistic expectations. It is time to re-evaluate your relationships, set boundaries and do not allow people to poison your spirit any longer! It may hurt to distance yourself, but just remember, you are really saving yourself from corruption, hurt and pain! My question is who is more important?

Reflections:

List the toxic person(s) in your life.

Identify what makes the person(s) on your list toxic.

What keeps you connected to the person(s) on your list?

What have they done to you that is considered unhealthy? How did it make you feel and how did you respond to their action(s)?

At what point will you know that you are ready to let go of the person, relationship?

How have you changed because of your interaction or relationship with the person(s)?

Are you a TOXIC person? If so, what characteristics do you possess?

Has anyone tried to help you grow from your ways? If so, how?

What do you attribute your toxic ways to?

What steps can you make to create a change in your daily walk and interactions with others?

LEARN

Recognize when a person reveals who they REALLY are! Do not get caught up in the representation that they put forth.

Everyone and I mean everyone has a representative. Yes, that means YOU too! What is a representative? A representative is the "fake" person you present when meeting someone that you do not know, or the persona you present when you are trying to form a relationship and are not sure about letting one "in" just yet. What happens is that most times we fall for the representative, because the representative says and does all of the right things. The representative is always "on". The representative is always making sure you never see them in a negative light and when that becomes exhausting, a slip in the perceived character happens. When this slip happens, we are so caught up in the "representative" that we overlook this revelation of who they really are. We must be careful when forming relationships. We must learn to use our wisdom, discernment, trust our instinct and pay attention to signs. Know that a person will always show you their true colors. It may be within a few days, or it may take weeks and months before you see the true essence of their character, but trust that the true self will be revealed when you least expect it. I once dated a guy that was all kinds of "right"! I mean he had everything on my mental rolodex check-list and I was on cloud nine.

As a one who earned a Master's degree in counseling, I began to notice that something was not quite right with this man. I knew he was respectful at times and could be very accommodating and thoughtful, but there was this Dr. Jekyll and Mr. Hyde quality about him. He would have random controlling outburst or would try to make me feel less than. He would always nitpick at my style or try to compare me to others, often. What made me finally take a good look at him and figure out what his diagnosis was, was the constant slip of being too good to be true and the random crazy outburst and narcissism. It began to be too much, and with that, I walked away. Your top priority should be your mental and emotional well-being. You must be on alert at all times and allow your spirit to recognize another's spirit for what it is and trust your instincts, because instincts are never wrong. We often second-guess ourselves because we are either willing to compromise due to loneliness or we truly believe we can fix someone. Know that these reasons are not good enough. You are your number one priority and you should protect your mental and emotional space as a top priority. Learn to look pass the representative and see what is truly within. Remember, everything always looks good on the outside, but once you see inside know that you have seen the truth.

Reflections:

Do you present a "representative" when meeting people? Why?

What does your "representative" look like?

Think about your past relationships, who did you become involved with that presented their representative and what characteristics did they exhibit? What made you end the relationship and were you aware of these signs in the dating stage?

What are "key" characteristics that you notice when people present their "representative"?

How can you protect your mental and emotional well-being when forming romantic or casual friendships?

LEARN

Some people are never to have starring, guest or recurring roles in the story of your life.

Imagine that someone is going to produce a movie based on your life and you have to include all the **zeros** you have ever dated. Sounds great, right? I mean all your bad, lonely, and irrational decisions to keep someone pass their expiration date. Yes, people have expiration dates relationally, physically, and spiritually! Makes for a great movie, huh? As a single woman or man, it can be hard to let go when it is time to LET GO and have the strength not go back, but that has not always been the case in some our lives. We enter into relationships and believe that we are "in love" and when the relationship ends, we venture into unhealthy practices of leaving the door open which causes emotional and mental distress. We will allow a faux relationship to continue because it gives us what we think we need or want, and even though we know that holding on is wrong, we allow the back and forth, in and out and emotional attachment to continue. Then we find it in us to date other people and when those relationships end, we allow them to remain dead; but for whatever reason, we hold reservation for the "one" we have allowed to manage our hearts.

This rollercoaster causes us pain mentally, emotionally, spiritually, and sadly physically. We begin to feel stuck and sad wondering when will we find or meet someone who truly wants us for who we are. But here is the newsflash, we are our own problem, not the one we desire, and we must put an end to their role of merry-go-round love. When we refuse to let go, move on, and keep people around longer than they need to be, we set ourselves up for failure. We have to learn to be cognizant of what we allow and mindful of our actions. We must realize that some people are never meant to be in your life. The saying "reason, season or lifetime" is so true. We usually know when a person's time is up or when we have had enough of their foolishness, and we know what we are doing when we allow the "in and out" to occur. But, in order for us to move forward, we have to have the strength to end relationships and walk away for good. We must pay attention to signs, feelings and changes that take place. We must learn to close chapters, learn from them and move on. Mariah Carey's "Butterfly", talks about letting a butterfly go and if it returns, then that is where they are supposed to be. We are like those butterflies and we have to learn to trust in the plan that God has for us.

Reflections:

Describe a relationship in which you held on for too long.

What was it about the person that caused you to continue to go back or stay?

Why did you choose to remain in a dead relationship?

Which area of your well-being suffered the most? How did you overcome?

What lesson(s) did you learn from the relationship and how did you grow from it?

LEARN

Age is just a number. If God gives you the vision, directions, and plans; He will ensure that it will happen. Remember, it is not over until God says it is over.

Who says you must have it all by the age of 30? No ONE! I know I most certainly do not. It is quite amazing to see associates, classmates and complete strangers start from the bottom making their way to the top. It fills me with pride and on the flipside, urgency. Why do I feel urgent, because I know that I wasted valuable years allowing fear and insecurities to defeat me? I become upset with myself each time I pick up a pad that has the same plan written in different ways. I feel like Jonah who tried to outrun God, but eventually went where God needed him to go in the end. There are many examples of successful people over 30 in the bible. The two that stand out are Abraham (Abram) and Sarah (Sarai). Abram had wealth, but no heir. His wife Sarai (Sarah) went outside the will of God, which resulted in him having a son, Ishmael with Hagar at the age of 68. After 31 years, God promised to make Abraham the father of many nations and told him he would bore a son. At age 100, Abraham and Sarah, 90, became parents to Isaac. God fulfilled every promise that he planned for them, even in the midst of them messing up. Now fast forward to the 20th century. We have many individuals who became successful after 40. Donald Fisher was 40 when he and his wife opened the first Gap store in 1969. Vera Wang was 40 when she designed her first gown. Samuel Jackson was 43 when he landed his breakout role in Spike Lee's film "Jungle Fever". Julia Child wrote her first book at the age of 50, which launched her career as a chef.

Deshun Wang, theatrical actor at 24, learned English at 44, started a pantomime troupe at 49, entered a gym for the first time at 50, at 57 returned to acting and created the world's only performance art called "Living Sculpture Performance", at 70 really became engrossed in working out and at the ripe age of 79 got his first catwalk! Can you say it is not over until God says it is over? Deshun Wang is still achieving and pushing the boundaries. He is still using his time left to go after the "potential". He has not given up, nor given in to the notion of his age holding him back. Wherever you are at this point in time in life, know that it is not over. Whatever you want to birth, make it happen. Whatever you desire, pursue it with passion. Age is merely a number. It is not the deciding factor of success. Your mindset, determination, passion and willingness to fail determine that. Nothing happens overnight. It will take hard work, consistency and dedication to birth what God has inside of you. You must be patient and stay the course. All of the individuals mentioned above started from somewhere else in life. Some had careers that prepared them for the victory ahead, and others did not. You do not have to be the expert, you just have to let the creativity flow and everything you need will come to you. My mantra is "Conceive it, Believe it, Achieve it"! If you can conceive an idea, you must believe in it to achieve it. It is all up to you!

Reflections:

What idea(s) have you put on the back burner?

What has stopped you from pursuing your vision/plan?

What support do you need to help you stay on track in bringing your vision/plan to life?

Take a sheet of paper, write down your vision/plan, steps needed to succeed and people who can hold you accountable. Ask those individuals to do weekly or monthly check-ins to monitor your progress. An accountability partner is a must!

If finances are holding you back from pursuing your vision/plan, what can you do right now to begin the process that is within your budget?

LEARN

To trust God with all things. Know that our human capacity can only see what is immediately before us. Remember, God sees it all.

Trust: firm reliance on the integrity, ability or character of a person or thing.

1. Custody; care.
2. Something committed into the care of another charge.
3. Reliance on something in the future.
4. To be confident in; depend on.
5. To believe

Are you trusting God? Have you given up control and placed yourself in His care? If not, today is the day! Know that God KNOWS all! He knows what is in your best interest. The definitions of *trust* show how your relationship with God should be. You must learn to place your faith and trust in Him to work things out for you. When you begin to leave Him out of the equation, your entire world turns upside down…literally! You begin to see things fall apart. You become frustrated and defeated because you are not seeing progress. You start to blame Him for things not coming together, forgetting you left Him out in the first place. Why do you go through this cycle? Simply put, you have decided to operate based on what you see and think. You have decided to use your near-sighted vision to make life decisions; but what can be done to help you get back on track and follow God's plan? As the definitions state, you must first place yourself in His custody and care and know that He will always provide what you need along the way. You must become committed and know that He is committed to ensuring you have your needs met daily. You must rely on Him for what is to come because you have no idea what tomorrow holds. You must be confident in His works and know that whatever happens and wherever He leads you is for your welfare. Lastly, you must, without doubt, BELIEVE!

Trusting God is believing in Him! It is believing He is your Protector! 2 Samuel 22:31 says "As for God, His way is perfect; the word of the Lord is tried, He is my shield to all those who trust and take refuge in Him." It is believing that He is your Stronghold! Psalm 91:2 says "I will say of the Lord, He is my Refuge and my Fortress, my God; on Him I lean and rely and in Him I trust!" It is believing He is your Provider! Matthew 6: 25-26 says, "Therefore I tell you, stop being perpetually uneasy about your life, what you shall eat *or what you shall drink*; or about your body, what you shall put on. Is not life greater than food, and the body than clothing? 26 Look at the birds of the air; they neither sow nor reap nor gather into barns, and yet your heavenly Father keeps feeding them. Are you not worth much more than they?" It is believing that He will Direct your path! Proverbs 3: 5-6, "Trust in and be confident in the Lord with all your heart and mind and do not rely on your own understanding, in all ways acknowledge Him and He will direct and make straight and plain your path."

It is believing He is the only one to Trust! Psalm 118:8, "It is better to trust in the Lord than to put confidence in man." It is believing that He will Deliver you as promised! Psalm 37:5, "Commit your way to the Lord; trust also in Him and He will bring it to pass." It is simply BELIEVING and trusting that all is well and that good will be done for your benefit. In a society that is losing faith, and trust becoming an obsolete word with man, you can know in your inner man that God will not fail and trusting in Him is a surety. Trusting God does not mean you cannot plan or act on your desires. It simply means that you involve God in your decisions and include Him in your action steps. It is seeking His directions and listening to your inner man. It is holding yourself accountable to follow through on what God has given you to do. Whatever you are going through or whatever the need, know that God has your back and he will not fail you! It is now time for you to put your trust in Him to meet your needs and deliver you from your trials. Remember, "a man's mind plans his way, but the Lord directs his steps and makes them sure" Proverbs 16:9. Are you ready to start trusting God to lead the way? Go ahead, take His hand and let Him take you to your blessings!

Reflections:

What areas in your life are you not trusting God?

If you are not trusting God, what is holding you back?

How have you trusted God before and how does this help you in current situations?

What does trusting God mean to you?

What are you believing God for?

Trusting God is having faith in His word. Where is your faith level? Are you operating on visual or spiritual faith? (Visual faith is relying on what you see transpiring in the natural. Spiritual faith is relying on the holy spirit to guide you even though you cannot see it; you know the manifestation will happen.)

What do you need to give over to God?

LEARN

That everyone does not want to be helped. Pray for them and let God do the rest.

Have you ever been around someone who has a complaining spirit? How about someone who is negative and drips in pessimism? I was created with a helping spirit, and have learned the hard way that everyone does not want help. The funny thing is I chose a career that involves helping people!! Crazy, right? Well as a graduate student taking my counseling courses, I learned that or rather realized that people already know what they have to do to change or move forward in life. We have a gauge that points us in the right direction, but sometimes people CHOOSE to wallow in despair, sin, hurt, and anger; therefore it takes a "want" or "desire" to move beyond that stage. I have learned to really listen to people and listen, not just with my ears, but with my eyes. You can talk until you are blue in the face, but when a person says one thing and actions show another; always go with the action. In the bible, there is a man in Bethesda who has been afflicted for some 38 years.

The parable goes that at an appointed time an angel would stir the waters and whoever enter the water after the stirring was healed. Jesus comes along and finds this certain man and when asked if he wanted to be healed, he does not immediately say yes, but gives an excuse as to why he is not healed yet. Maybe someone else may read that and receive differently, but my spirit says he answered with an excuse. Sometimes when we try to help people, they tend to give us all the reasons as to why they have not been successful in helping themselves, when that is not the question on the table. The question is do you want to be helped? And many times, that answer is no. Sometimes people are not ready to move forward. They have become used to complaining and sharing their sob tale, and when someone comes along to help them, they are not ready to accept it or change. One thing I have learned is that when a person is ready to change or ready to receive help, they usually make the first step. We, on the outside, have to learn to let people go. We have to learn that when we offer our help and it is not wanted to move on and not force the issue.

Help is both a noun and verb. As a noun it is the action of one doing for another and as a verb it is serving or giving assistance. We, those on the outside, are the verbs in a person's life. We see what they need and want to give it to them, but they must truly want and accept the help offered. As much as it hurts us to be declined, we have to know it is not that person's time to receive help, or the help is not to come from you, nor I. So, to my helpers out there, move on. When your support, assistance and aid is declined, do not take it personally. Do not get upset with the person and write them off. Do not speak ill of them, instead pray that they will get what they need in due time. Once you have prayed, it is time to let that relationship expire because it will become taxing to be with or around a person who needs help but is not in the place to receive it. Yes, this might hurt, but to salvage the relationship there must be a break and you must love, care and watch that person from afar.

Many may not agree, but for your own well-being emotionally and mentally, removing yourself from the situation is crucial. Secondly, give advice when it is asked for. Yes, I know, "but my friends love my advice!" No, they do not, especially when it is not asked for. Helpers have to learn to help and give advice when it is asked for. I catch myself all the time and stop in my tracks. I have learned, and it has taken a minute, to keep my mouth closed. If my friend or family member does not ask, I have nothing to give anymore. People only want to hear your advice when they already know what decision they are going to make, and they just want someone, anyone to side with them. Think about that for a second. Very rarely will someone change their mind, but advice is just that, advice, people can take it or leave it. So, from this point forward, learn to read your friends and family. Learn to not take their decline for help personally, instead give it to God and move on.

Reflections:

Who have you tried to help, but was declined? What reasons did the person give? How did it make you feel?

Have you declined help? If so, why? How did you help yourself or has the issue not been resolved?

In what way(s) do you offer help to others?

When your help has been declined, how does it make you feel? How is the relationship after the decline?

Who are the helpers in your life? What contributions or impacts have they made on your life?

What do you need help with now?

How do you plan to overcome the problem? List your steps.

LEARN

From your mistakes. Every mistake is an opportunity for growth!

No one is perfect, and no one expects perfection from you! You are allowed to make mistakes. Mistakes build character. Mistakes create experiences. Mistakes are great opportunities for growth. Some people condemn themselves for making mistakes by continuously reliving it. They harp on the mistakes or failures, continue to speak about it to others and rest in the emotional stress that it causes. One must take mistakes for what they are; not regret them. You must see pass the mistake. Mistakes teach you where you went wrong and leads you to make better decisions in the future. Mistakes are simply life lessons. Sometimes people allow mistakes to take them down negative paths of depression, partaking in drugs and alcohol to cope or continuous condemnation. The bible is filled with examples of people making mistakes and being used for something greater. One of those is Moses. Moses made the mistake of killing another man. Exodus 2:11-15 speaks of how Moses, upon seeing his brethren being assaulted and persecuted by an Egyptian, goes to defend his brethren and in the process killed the Egyptian and hid him. The next day, he saw his brethren fighting each other and one confronts one of them about fighting each other, but the man turns to Moses and speaks of his crime. After Moses's crime is exposed, he hides in another land for years reconciling with his sin; and although he committed this crime defending another, God still had a plan to use him for a greater purpose.

Peter denied Jesus three times and condemned himself; but picked himself up so that he could continue to do the work of preaching and teaching. Mistakes are meant for you to overcome. Mistakes are meant for you to overcome and grow from so that you can teach others. They teach you how to forgive yourself allowing you to see God's grace in the aftermath. Owning up to your mistakes sets you free. I have been there. I have wallowed in my sins, mistakes, and beat myself up. I have been in a low place and did not want to forgive myself, but in order to grow and move forward, I had to allow God to remove the pain and be my focus to move on. In so doing, I was able to let go and grow. I was able to help someone else through the same situation to live freely. One thing that helps me navigate through my life's mistakes is having an accountability partner. When you have someone, you trust and can depend on to be honest, nonjudgmental and cares for you unconditionally, it makes dealing with live in the present much easier. Whatever you have done, or decisions made, know that it is not end. Pick yourself up and decide to move forward in the lesson learned so that you do not go back again.

Reflections:

What mistake held you hostage, not allowing you to set yourself free?

How did you overcome the pain or guilt from the mistake(s) made?

What lessons were learned from your mistakes?

How have your grown from your mistakes?

How has your testimony helped another in the same situation?

How do you handle mistakes today?

Have you ever considered having an accountability partner? Why or why not?

LEARN

As you mature in your spiritual walk, you must leave some things and people behind.

As you mature in your spiritual walk, your way of thinking, ways of living and what you deem important changes. That is just the natural course of life. During my teenage years, I longed to understand the word and apply it to my life. I was not necessarily doing things I should not, but I was by no means a sweet little angel. I read the bible sometimes, which usually consisted of reading Revelations, my favorite book of the bible and of course prayed, but it was generic and basic. I simply did not have a mature relationship. When I entered young adulthood, I rarely went to church, because I did not find one I liked near my college, but still prayed and read the bible with little understanding. Upon graduating from college, I began to have a need to know more and understand the bible. I began to regularly attend my home church, and I began to pray for the words to come to life to me. I began reading the "Left Behind" series because it focused on my favorite book, Revelations. Some may think that I was crazy for diving head first into this series, but reading this series, not going to church on a regular basis, created a desire to mature in my walk. The series had me reading the bible to "fact check" and it opened my eyes to me needing to get my life in order. I remember it like yesterday. I was in my room at my parents' house studying and praying for God to allow the words to resonate in my spirit and it happened. From that moment on, my walk changed.

I began working on my character, mouth, attitude and who I surrounded myself with. I stopped doing things just to do them and held myself to a high standard of setting an example for others. I got involved in ministry and hung out less. I stopped buying liquor to make those "stress-reliever" drinks at home. I stopped talking to certain people because their focus was not mine, and I stopped going out as much and began to focus more on my purpose. Now, my circle is small. I most certainly do not do things I used to do, nor am I entertained by them. Some people say the bible does not say you cannot do this or that, but my response is how are you acting in certain situations? Are you looking like you are a part of the world or set apart? There is nothing wrong with good, clean fun with people who honor your walk; but when they do not, it is time to remove yourself from them because you will eventually fall. Maturing in your walk is growth. It is realizing there is more to life, and you want the more. It is a positive move in the right direction. It is releasing those who are not moving in your direction. It is disconnecting from things that will hinder and set you back. We all know that at a certain time in our lives we let people go and that is due to maturing. Therefore, it is no different with your spiritual walk. As you grow spiritually, you need people in your life who are growing and understand the support you will need. You will need unconditional and nonjudgmental support, and will come to realize that everyone is not meant to be in your life forever. Therefore, the saying of a person being in your life for a reason, season or lifetime is indeed true and something you must learn to recognize if you wish to be successful in your walk.

Reflections:

Have you started the process of maturing in your spiritual walk? If so, how? If not, what is holding you back?

Who will or is your support system?

What steps are you taking to mature in your spiritual growth?

What makes this person(s) a good candidate to support you?

What things have you let go of?

What are you still holding on to?

Why are you still holding on?

Who have you let go of in order to mature in your walk?

Why did you have to leave this person(s) behind?

What is your fear of letting go of these things or people?

LEARN

*Procrastination equals Disobedience.
When God says "do" or "go, get it
done in His time, not yours.*

Many of you know the biblical story of Jonah. Jonah is like many of us. We are given a word, vision, or task to do and we run from it or take our time in following through. In the book of Jonah, Jonah was told to go to Nineveh and proclaim against the wickedness of the city. Instead of following what the Lord had spoken to him, Jonah left and went in the opposite direction far from where the Lord wanted him to go. Many times, when we are given an assignment from the Lord we tend to run or procrastinate, which are actions of disobedience. We are willfully disobeying the Lord. It is like telling your parent "You cannot tell me what to do" or simply ignoring them. Think back to a time when your parent asked or told you to do something around the house and you took your sweet time, what happened? Was your parent pleased or displeased? Did they threaten to "get" you or scold you for not obeying? Sure, they did, because you were being disobedient. The story continues with Jonah sneaking onto a ship and as he is out to sea, a violent storm comes about. The men on the ship began to pray to their gods to no avail. They find Jonah, find out who he serves and casts lots finding out he is the cause of their troubles. Jonah suggests the unthinkable; throw him out to sea. The men oblige, and the violent winds cease.

You see when we procrastinate, we tend to get involved in other things that take us away from our purpose. It interferes with the plan the Lord has for us leading us to make rash decisions about new situations we have placed ourselves. We become frustrated and upset wondering why things are not working out for us, never owning up to the fact we are at fault. Now after being thrown into the sea, the Lord had a great fish to swallow Jonah and he remained in the belly of fish for three days and nights. Amid our derailment, God still uses us to reach others. I have mentioned this before, but I will mention it again, during my procrastination period, God used me to lead a group of women in a small group. Although I had not started my girls' mentoring group or written my book, He still used me to reach others along my road of disobedience. During this time God was preparing and molding me. He was getting me back on track and building my confidence. He was erasing my fears and providing me with experiences to draw upon. He was carefully crafting my skill to teach, speak and reach! He was teaching me how to pray and I developed a stronger relationship with Him. I began to blog in the midst. I created a girls' mentoring group at my school. I became involved in an array of ministries. I grew in my faith and gifts. I became an online Christian radio host.

Just like Jonah, who was placed right back where God wanted him to go, I eventually found my way back to the purpose and vision God had given me 6 years ago. I have learned in the process that procrastination is disobedience and it causes you to take years from your years of success. I am always thinking to myself, you should be much further along", but because I decided to do things in *my* time, I have added time that should not be there. I pushed my blessings back. I put a halt to my story. Jonah made it to Nineveh and did as the Lord instructed him to do. He spoke against the city and prophesied, which led the people to believe and repent. In procrastinating, Jonah caused the city to continue to live in sin, until he got his mind right about being obedient and doing the work of the Lord. In my procrastination, I have not used my gifts the way God wanted me to, to bless and uplift others who might have needed a word of inspiration or support. I say all this to say, whatever God has called you to do, STOP running and START obeying. It is time to walk in your destiny. It is time to walk in your purpose. It is time to do what you were born to do. Push fear aside. Push your inadequacies to the side. Know that the Lord will not call you do anything that He has not prepared the way. Do not become jaded in the process of obeying as Jonah did. Know that the will of God is the ultimate goal and you, we, are here to fulfill it.

Reflections:

What are you procrastinating in doing for God?

How do feel about being disobedient?

How is it affecting your walk?

Why are you procrastinating?

What plans will you put in place to ensure you complete the plan God has for you?

During your procrastination stage, how are you preparing to do what God has called you to do?

LEARN

Never limit God-He has NO boundaries! God can rearrange any circumstance in your favor!

In life, we will encounter situations beyond our control and when this happens we are used to viewing it from one lens, one that does not always show a way to move beyond or other routes to take. But as we mature in our spiritual walk, we learn that God is in control and situations can be turned around for our favor in an instant. A perfect example of this is Genesis 37-50 because it speaks of how life can be good, turn for the worse and in the end, you come out on top. Joseph was his father's favorite and was given a coat specifically made for him. On top of being the favorite, Joseph had the gift of prophesying. Joseph told everyone his latest dream, that they would bow to him and of course this made his older brothers furious, keep in mind they were already jealous of him, so when has hate and jealousy ever done good? Well as one would have it, the older brothers conspired to do away with Joseph. They put him in a pit, covered the coat with blood and sold him into slavery. I am going to pause here. I want you to think about a time in your life where the odds were against you. What went through your head? Who or what halted your progress? Who or what aided your progress? You see, in life we will be met with obstacles in the form of people or things, but we must know that it is not what we see in the present, but what we know and believe is our end. God has placed in each one of us a gift to help others.

Sometimes the gift will not be well received as it was with Joseph, and individuals will conspire against us, but we must not lose faith in using it. Now, let's continue with Joseph. Joseph enters Egypt and works in the master's house and found favor in his sight. Lesson here is even when the situation looks bleak, God will give you favor and hope to keep you striving to the end. Although Joseph ran in to trials, he came out on top due to continuing to walk in his gift and relying on the Lord to get him through. This reminds me of my time as a testing coordinator and

I simply hated it. As mentioned before, I literally wanted to quit my job, but I had to remember who I worked for, and who was in control. You must do the same as well. In the end, Joseph saved his family and became a leader. He came out on top because he was always with God. Whatever the situation or circumstance, know that God is the orchestrator. Know that when it looks bad and you cannot see a way through, stay in God's presence and listen to His directions. You may be down and out tomorrow, but lo and behold, in the morning you may be singing a new song. Pray. Trust. Believe.

Reflections:

Describe a time in which a situation looked bad, but God turned it around for the good.

In the situation described above, when did you decide to relinquish control?

What favor was granted?

How did God turn it around and when did you recognize it?

Describe the emotions you felt in the situation.

What did you learn about yourself?

Are you currently in a situation that seems bleak, no way out or overwhelming? If so, write a prayer asking God to reveal himself as the orchestrator and be specific about your needs. Ensure you are trusting God, believing in His power, and stay committed to your walk and prayer life during this time.

LEARN

God will bless and surround you with a support team. He will place people in your life who will STAND with you. You are NOT alone!

I am a firm believer in destiny. I believe that we are all here in a space in time living and pursuing the ideas and life that has been birthed in us. I believe that things just do not happen, and people do not cross our paths haphazardly. True friends are a rarity! They are in my opinion hard to come by, but when you get that one true friend, hold on tight. During a fasting period, I was led to read Daniel and I learned so many mini lessons that month. One of those lessons happens to be this "learn". Daniel had strong, likeminded individuals in his clique. They prayed together and stayed true to the word of God. They possessed the qualities of friendship we all want. They trusted Daniel and he trusted them. They were supportive and when Daniel succeeded, they succeeded as well. They literally had his back, and he, theirs. They were in sync and took a stand when the time was needed. I have been blessed to have some great friends. They have been there for me on many occasions. One that stands out is during my test coordinating days. I knew I was going to be at the school for an "all-nighter". I was frustrated due to lack of support and absolutely over the task. School was well over and we were going on 7:00p.m. when one of my friends came in. She saw the despair and frustration on my face, placed her bags down and jumped right in. She talked me down from my high level of stress and spoke words of encouragement. She kept a lively conversation going that had nothing to do with work and even thought of a better system of getting our task done. When we finished our task, she stayed and asked if there was anything else and of course there was, but I did not want to have her with me all night.

Well the decision was not mine. She stayed with me and my teammate and helped us until almost 12:00 a.m. that morning. Her selflessness was admirable and appreciated. She stepped in because she knew my work ethic and how once I start, I must finish. She saved me and my teammate that night, because the two of us were not going to get it done by ourselves. She and I are alike in that we take pride in what we do and want everything to go as seamless as possible for others. God knew I needed her in my life and that day was already written in the book for us. You see, God knows all our hiccups and halting moments. He knows that we will need people to help us get through different seasons and places those people in our lives. He knows who will stay a lifetime and who will casually pass through. He knows who will be true and who will not. He did not design us to be alone on this journey, therefore when we meet people, pray about their place in your life. Pray that He reveals why you two or three have come together and honor the relationship. Pray with and for your friends. Stand with them and minister to their spirit in time of need. Learn them, know their ways, wants, innermost desires, and hold them accountable. Just like Daniel (Belteshazzar), Hananiah (Shadrach), Mishael (Meshach), and Azariah (Abednego), stay true to yourself and your friendship, respect one another, be transparent with each other, pray together, and stand up and support your friend in their time of need and despair. You are not alone, and your journey has hidden treasures of support already lined up waiting for you.

Reflections:

Who is your "clique"? (group of friends that have your back, stand up and pray for you).

What qualities does each person possess?

How did you meet your friends?

Describe a time in which your friend or friends have been there for you. What did you appreciate the most?

What type of friend are you?

Describe a time in which you have been there for your friend(s).

Read the book of Daniel. What stands out to you about the friendship between Daniel, Shadrach, Meshach, and Abednego?

How does your friendship(s) resemble theirs?

What can you do to be a better support system?

Pray and meditate asking God to reveal your place in your friends lives.

LEARN

Being rejected hurts, but God knows better. Therefore, do not run from rejection. The sting may hurt, but the pain will build an armor of protection.

"Raise your hands in the air and wave them like you just don't care. If you've ever been hurt by someone you love, let me hear you say, OH YEAH!" Okay, I know that may sound really corny, but it is true. We have all been hurt by someone we hold dear, love and respect. It is the nature of the game of life. Rejection is a hard pill to swallow. The pain is real and the hurt runs deep. It is amazing that emotional pain hurts the same as physical pain, and no one ever prepares you for it. In the 2013 "Psychology Today" article by Guy Winch, he lists 10 facts about rejection and one of those facts states that rejection triggers the same areas of the brain as physical pain. The same signals are sent and hence the hurt. Often when we are rejected we begin to look at ourselves to try and figure out how we, the individual person, went wrong. We begin to blame ourselves for the failure or lack of sustainability and beat ourselves up emotionally by reliving the event over and over. Sometimes this hurt, pain is so detrimental that it causes or leads some to depression, suicidal thoughts or worse, murder. I speak to students about this every year and without fail, I have students who make faces or laugh because teens decide to take their lives due to a breakup of a relationship.

I explain to them that this is a real pain, one in which a person feels they cannot come out of. I liken it to adults, who on the other end of the spectrum become angry and take their aggression out by deciding to take another person's life. In both instances, rational thought has been lost and psychological damage has been done. Rejection is the dismissing or refusing of a proposal, idea; the spurning of a person's affections. We were created to be among others, to live, work and have connections. When those connections die, we must rewire our brains to accept it and move on. Although rejection hurts, we must separate the pain from the lesson and use the pain to make us stronger. Yes, being rejected is hard, I know from experience, but I refused to allow the pain to consume me. I spoke positively to myself in those hard moments and gave myself a time limit to "wallow". I refused to be consumed by the hurt. I allowed myself 3 days to hurt, cry, ask, relive, be angry, cry again and then I was over it. I had to be. I could not continue to wonder why, but come to an understanding that it was not to be. And this is where people have a hard time. Letting go!

We must understand that when rejection occurs, that season or reason is over with and we should have come out with a life "nugget". We must understand that everything and everyone is not for us. We must learn that through rejection, we learn about ourselves and what we need to come out as the victor. I view rejection as a tool to overcoming. It is essential to building up our emotional muscles and learning how to adjust to a new reality. It helps us build barriers and boundaries that teach us to be more aware of our interactions with others. It makes way for us to build our self-esteem and learn new routes of moving on. We can choose to view rejection as a shot to the heart, or as a means of protection in the end. I choose protection. I see it as saving me from undue stress and more pain. I choose to see it as a power move that puts me in the advantage of allowing space for someone or something else to make way that is better for me. I choose to not allow rejection to destroy me. What do you choose?

Reflections:

This section may be hard to complete due to rehashing past hurts. If you are not strong enough or capable, do not reflect.

How do/did you handle rejection outside of an amorous relationship?

How have you handled rejection from someone you have love(d)?

What negative self-talk do/did you participate in?

How did you overcome your emotional pain?

If you have not overcome your emotional pain, what steps will you take to heal and move forward?

What lessons have you learned about yourself with dealing with rejection?

What boundaries have you set for yourself to help deal with rejection in the future?

LEARN

To give thanks and praise in all
things no matter the circumstance.

Have you ever been so low that you did not see a way out? Have you ever suffered from an illness and no matter who you saw, or medicines taken, you never got better? Have you ever been in a financial crisis and could not see the light of day? I wager to say the answer is yes to these. We have all been in a situation or have had circumstances that have tested our faith, trust, and belief system. We have doubted, cried, been frustrated, and have given up hope in some instances that things will work out for the better. We have all been there! But we have not all handled it the same way. In the infancy of my spiritual walk, I used to solely focus on my problems. I would allow my circumstances to consume me, which led to health issues with my digestive system, as well as my mental and emotional state of mind. I could not get pass the "why" and would drown in defeat. I had not learned how to view my life and the circumstances that would arise from a higher perspective. I could not see the positives or victories ahead and truthfully, none of us can when we continuously keep our eyes on our problem.

But, as I began to mature in my walk, I learned that those circumstances were preparing me for other events that would occur later in life. I learned that if I focused on the negative, the problem, the situation; I would never see my victory, nor pray and seek guidance from the Lord. I learned that by focusing on others, praying for others, and lifting others up in my time of need, helped me to see that my problem was not great at all in comparison to someone else. I began to speak life in to my circumstances and to thank God for allowing me to go through them because in the end, I would have the victory. I began to praise and speak the word of God to my problems and circumstances. And in praising and thanking, I became elevated to a more positive view of my situations. In praising you experience joy and peace of mind. You feel the weight of your problems being lifted and can enjoy your life in the now, regardless of the heavy presence of the present. In thanking and praising, you see the hand of God move mightily because you are placing your trust in the One who sees all and knows the outcome, but this is a process. We need to intentionally begin to thank and praise God in our situations and circumstances. We must learn to claim victory over it. What do I mean by that?

When I had stomach issues, I was angry and upset that I was "sick". I could not understand why I had to go through the pain and discomfort, but when I finally accepted that I had a health issue, I began to speak against and claim victory over it, instead of going with it. I began to thank God for healing and restoration of what He designed in me. I began to defeat the negative thought patterns by finding alternatives to medicines and foods to consume. I began to thank and praise God for placing me in the hands of a professional who would listen and diagnose correctly. I became active in my healing! I chose to praise God through it all because not doing so, would keep me defeated and sick. I am always reminded of Hannah from the Bible. Hannah could not bear a child, but she believed, thanked and praised God during her infertility. She never gave in to the idea that this was her fate and her circumstance was the final answer. No, she claimed her fertility. She believed in it and remained steadfast in knowing that it would one day be resolved, and sure enough that day came! Hannah bore Samuel and dedicated her blessing back to the Lord and had 5 more children after that. Hannah did not give up! She stayed committed to her praise. She stayed committed to the belief that God is able, because no matter her circumstance at the time, she knew she had the victory! Whatever your circumstance or situation is, start praising God now! Know that your thanksgiving and praise are well received. Know that the circumstance you are dealing with is temporal and will have a greater meaning as your testimony for those who will need to hear it in the future. Know that you are not alone, and the victory is yours!

Reflections:

Describe a time in which you were hard pressed and did not see an out. What actions did you display during this time and what emotions did you experience?

Describe a time in which you thanked and praised God during a situation/circumstance. What was the outcome of your situation?

How has thanking and praising God during a time of need helped you deal with the situation?

When you are praising and thanking God, what feelings do you experience?

What has thanking and praising God during a circumstance taught you?

LEARN

God has something better in store for you! Know your worth!

So, you've been "in love", and then something happens; nothing bad, but maybe it was the timing, an unfortunate circumstance, death or maybe there was an agreed upon decision to walk away, but your heart was not ready to let go. How do you handle that? What do you do? The heart is a very tricky machine. Yes, I call it a machine. It works like one, but the idea of the heart loving and longing is a beast! It can rule your world by making you happy, sad, excited, warm, loved and the list can go on and on; but, how do you get your heart on the same page as your mind? You must decide to release it! Let go of what you are holding on to and breathe again! For years, I used to struggle with letting go and truth be told, when you love someone, break down your barriers and finally let them in it is hard to do. But when you are finally ready to accept and receive the blessing God has in store for you, you then know that you have matured. You have grown. You see, it is hard for the "flesh" to comprehend the spirit's reasoning for releasing your heart, especially when we THINK, we KNOW what is BEST for us. But I have come to realize that I, nor you, know a thing! God knows ALL and how ALL will turn out, so when He shows us the way out, we need to take heed and walk through that door of a better opportunity and new connections. Letting go means RELEASING. We must release the hurt, pain, love, memories, bitterness, hardness, and any other emotion we have attached to the object of our affections to RECEIVE what God has in store for us. It took me a long to time get to a point of understanding this. For years, I stood in my own way, not allowing God to move. I hindered my future and missed opportunities to connect with someone who could have possibly been my future due to me hanging onto my feelings and not allowing my heart to be free. When you are truly ready to release you might experience a combination of peace and sadness. The peace will come from knowing that you are ready to move forward, and the sadness will come from the divorce of the relationship. Do not become caught up in your emotions and attachment. By doing so, you will never find the strength to leave. To help you in the process of releasing your heart, you must do a few things:

1. Put your utmost faith in God.
2. Allow God to lead your heart and mind in His direction.
3. Let go of physical reminders that will cause you to turn back.
4. Cut off contact so that God can strengthen you to move forward.
5. Rebuke any thoughts that come up to challenge your growth.
6. Thank God for the blessing he has in store for you.

Will this task be easy for your flesh? NO, but with God leading the way and you remaining out of the way, all will be well. I hope that you recognize the signs of a dead relationship. I hope that you open yourself up to God and allow Him to control your destiny. I pray you find strength in Him and remember that He has your best interest at hand. It is time to release, so that you can receive!

Reflections:

Why do you believe that you deserve better? If you believe this, what makes you stay in an unhealthy relationship?

Think of a past relationship. What situation(s) caused you to leave? How long did it take for you to release your heart?

What has stopped you from letting go?

If you are in a current relationship that is not meeting your needs, what do you need to pray for to help you release your heart, so that you may move on?

List your past relationships and the reasons you moved on and how long it took for you to release your heart. Do you notice a pattern? If so, what changes do you need to make when deciding to commit to a relationship?

~Prayer~

Father, I thank you for loving, guiding, teaching, and never forsaking me. Lord, I thank you for the lessons that life brings to grow and help me mature in my spiritual walk. Lord, I praise you for every situation and circumstance that has caused me pain. In that pain, I know that I have grown and learned more about myself, but most importantly, you! Lord help me to recognize the spirits of others and to protect myself from their toxicity. Lord help me to let go of situations out of my control and place them in your hands. Father, help me to discern people's spirits and lead me to those you have placed in my life to help. Lord, I thank you for time! Lord, I thank you for the vision you have birthed in me and pray that I will not be a hindrance to myself. Lord, forgive me for at times limiting your power. Help me to stay out of my way and allow you to do you! Father, I pray you will surround me with a support team that has the love of Christ in their hearts who want to walk in your light. Father, forgive me for procrastinating. Help me to keep my mind on you, focus my thoughts, bless me with accountability partners and hear your voice. Lord, I thank you, praise you, lift your name up on high for you are the King of Kings and Lord of Lords. In Jesus's name, I pray. Amen!

~Affirmation~

I am a child of Christ and in me I have the power bestowed upon me through the Holy Spirit. I will learn from the life lessons that come my way. I will learn to listen to the Holy Spirit and allow the Holy Spirit to guide me in my walk. I am blessed and highly favored. I have the strength to walk away from situations that are not healthy for me. I will use my discernment to see the heart of individuals who come into my life. I will no longer hold on to my wants when they are not in the will of God. I will allow God to lead and direct

126

my footsteps. I will be caution of who I allow in my space. I am a conqueror over all situations and circumstances. I have the victory through Christ Jesus and will praise Him in all I do. I will release my heart and guard my mind against those who try to harm me. I will place my confidence in you and encourage myself when I feel low. I am prosperous in all that I do, and I will commit to the purpose you have birthed in me. I will not limit myself, nor will I continue to live in bondage. I am free. I am loved. I am who God says I am!

Life is meant to be lived! We should enjoy each moment we are alive to take a breath, because we do not know when it will be our last. Many of us simply live. We live life never caring to learn from life's trials. We place ourselves in the same situations over and over and begin to blame God and complain about how life "just isn't fair!" Then we have those who live and learn! They make mistakes, learn from the them, and do everything in their power to never return to the former. That is called growth. When life's journey takes us down a rocky road, we pick up the lessons and notate them in our journal of life. We pay attention to signs others exhibit. We pay attention to how we handle situations and adjust; and that is what growing is all about. Growing means you begin to see the world from a clear lens, not the oh so lovely "rose-colored" one. You begin to not be selfish and believe the world revolves around you. You mature mentally and spiritually! Growing "up" is an essential part of life, but everyone does not grow at the same rate. The time has come to "grow". The time has come to learn life's lesson. The time to grow is now because tomorrow is not promised. It is time to grow from your life's experiences!

"Just because you're grown, doesn't mean you've grown."- Dedra Colston

It's time to GROW

GROW

Growing in specific areas of your life must be cultivated. Plant, water, place in the SON, and see the beauty that springs from it.

Have you ever tried to grow something, such as a plant or vegetable? If so, did you succeed or fail? I must admit that I am not good when it comes to planting a seed and giving it the things it needs to flourish. I am absolutely not good at it and have given up on ever trying to do it. Have you had the opportunity to watch a newborn child grow from an infant to an adolescent or adult? I have had this pleasure as a proud aunt and an educator, and truly believe the growth process is amazing! But when it comes to my life, when it comes to growth, I can be all in or lukewarm. I can set out knowing what I need and how to get there to get started only to be sidetrack with notes and agendas that have been misplaced here and there. On the other hand, I can buckle down and stay focused and reap the harvest of my labor to get from point A to B. The thing is, when you want to change something about yourself, you must be committed to the change or growth. You must make up your mind to be committed by being consistent and staying with the plan no matter what curveballs life throws. But how many times do you start and fail? How often do you start with good intention by "planting" the idea in your mind and jotting down action steps to end up giving in not even a week later? The answer is, too often.

Growing is not easy. It is not this magical notion of saying it and it happens. It is not a "write the plan and it will be" type of notion. Growth is being intentional and that takes work. To grow, you must first identify, or "plant", what you want to change for the better and how you see yourself in the end. I love Stephen Covey's quote, "begin with the end in mind", because it is setting the scene. It is focusing your mind on a specific outcome which prompts you to make strides in that direction. Once the idea is firmly planted one must become cognizant of the obstacles and prepare your mind for the challenges ahead. In order to prepare, you must know your pitfalls and patterns and off set them with the right environment. Setting the right environment is crucial to being successful in your growth. The right environment means you will have the right support and energy needed to be successful. It is surrounding yourself with positive influences, feeding your thoughts with positivity and inspiration, having accountability partners and changing your attitude in order to make the transformation. Along with setting the right environment, you must feed your spirit and mind with the right information and word by meditating and spending time in prayer for direction that will empower you to be your best self.

You must know that greater is in you and that you are meant to live a prosperous life. Growth can be hard, especially when your flesh is fighting against you and you are leaving people behind, because let's face it, when you grow, you tend to lose friends and associates who were only around you because you were not going anywhere beyond "them". You were in the same boat with them and when you make the decision to do and be better, you will rebel against yourself. Yes, YOU will rebel against yourself, because with "growing up" comes "growing pains", and we do not like to experience pain. That is why meditating on the word of God, praying, and setting the right environment is crucial to your success. As a child, my father was in the world. He did what the average male did, but he came to a point in his life where he knew he had to place his family on the top of his priority list and that meant changes had to be made. My father stopped hanging around his old friends and he told them why. He let go of dead weight and allowed his spirit man to lead. He became more involved in church, which led to finding a church home that fed him exactly what he needed to honor the role in which he had been given, head of household.

He focused on our family and set examples for us. He grew as a man and father before my eyes. Did it take work? YES! Did he have to let go to gain more? YES! Did he have to change his mind and surround himself with positive influences? YES! Did he reap a harvest? YES! His marriage grew stronger! His work opportunities expanded for the better, and his children grew in the knowledge of the Lord and were successful. And if you were to ask him was his growth experience worth it? His answer would be "YES!" Do not be afraid to grow. Do not be afraid of what will be left behind. The time has come to throw out the old you and grow into what you were born to do. It is time to grow from old ways and live life anew. It is time to stretch and reach for more. It is time for you to GROW!

Reflections:

Think about where you are right now in your life. In what area(s) do you need to grow?

What do you need to do to get started?

Who do you need to let go of to be successful?

Who will be your accountability partners?

Which scriptures will give you the support you need to make this growth a reality?

What changes do you need to make to be successful?

To assist you in keeping track start a journal of your progress and reflect on it weekly.

GROW

Pray for those that persecute you.

This grow comes straight from Matthew 5:44. The complete verse reads starting with verse 43 "You have heard that it was said, You shall love your neighbor and hate your enemy; 44 But I tell you, Love your enemies and pray for those who persecute you"- The Amplified Bible

As humans, our human nature 9 times out of 10, usually tells us to dislike or hate those who wrong us. Our minds create scenarios of how we can seek revenge, or we use our mouths to speak ill of the person to everyone we know. We even go as far as to teach our children to fight back and return the same rudeness and ill-treatment to those that wrong them. But how is this helpful and where does this normally lead? I will tell you that it leads to hatred, anger, unresolved issues, fights and more. This verse is the epitome of growth! It is simply going higher and choosing to be the better person, and in the famous words of Michelle Obama, "when they go low, we go high!" I know there will be push back on this one and it is okay. But for just a moment I want you to indulge me. Indulge me on the idea that by choosing to go higher, you will feel better about you and the situation. It will not be a constant thought and a strategic game of chess to seek revenge. You will have the upper hand, because your "enemy" will be trying to figure out why you have not had a comeback or attacked them in some form or fashion.

It will leave them in a state of wonder. Your enemy, someone who is against you or threatens you in some way, is one who means to cause strife in your life. By *choosing* to allow your enemy to do this to you is all on you! The verse is quite simple, but learning how to go higher is hard when it seemingly goes against your flesh. But here is the key, we must learn that we are not fighting against flesh, but against principalities, spirits, and when you realize that you must pray. You must give up living by the flesh and allow your spirit and the holy spirit to reign! Praying for your enemies becomes easy when you realize they do not have the last word. Praying for your enemies is praying for them to see the errors of their ways. It is praying that God will reveal himself to them and give you the strength to press on despite what they are trying to do to you. It is praying that the truth of their nature will be revealed to those that need to see it and you will be seen in a brighter light. It is praying that God will be your recompense and the victory will be yours! This "grow" is vital! It is vital because we are living in a time where people of faith will be persecuted for their beliefs. It is happening every day in other parts of the world, but in America it is picking up steam.

Christians are being persecuted daily and it is nasty. Christians are being pulled into dialogue that is exposing their maturity level in their walk and we are failing. We are failing because we are responding in some cases in the same nastiness and rudeness as the enemy. As a Christian, we must realize that the battle is not ours and choose to respond in the correct manner. We must step out of the flesh and allow the spirit to work and we must be consistent. There is a student at my school that walks in this every day. He has been persecuted day after day, week after week, month after month and year after year for the past 3 years. I have watched him keep a smile and sometimes cry, but he has stood strong. Recently, he was punched in the face by another student and instead of retaliating, he simply went to the nurse's office. He did not seek revenge, nor did he press assault charges. He came to my office and we talked. I asked him how he felt and what surprised me was that he did not respond like someone who had just been physically attacked. He gave me a half smile and said, "I'll be fine. It hurts a little, but I just want to sit here for a while." We talked about his feelings and I told him it was okay if he were upset. He simply said "I do not know why he hit me. Miss, I was not talking to him, and I don't want to fight or get him in trouble."

We talked some more before he returned to class, but before

he left he told me that his parents did not want him fighting back, instead, they wanted him to walk away from his bullies, "his enemies". They did not want him to end up like his brother. In a way, I am glad that his parents are teaching him not to fight, but on the flipside, I wonder if they have really equipped him with how to stand and handle the persecution. And that is the key! We must equip ourselves with the right information to stand up, walk away and pray for our enemies. We must meditate on the word, build-up our self-esteem and confidence, and most importantly we must know without a doubt who we are in Christ. I cannot talk about faith with my student in the public arena, but I do pray for my student. I pray that he is strengthen and will not fall prey to the attacks that can take place in his mind. I pray that his parents are feeding him the word he needs to continue to stand strong, and I will continue to pray for his enemies for him! So, I leave you with this…do not be dismayed. Do not be tempted to seek the ways of the flesh! Instead, STAND strong and firmly planted on the word of God and know He has your back and the victory is yours against your enemies! Pray for them and watch the Holy Spirit do its work!

Reflections:

Describe a time an enemy persecuted you?

What emotions did you feel?

What were the first thoughts that came to mind in responding to the attack?

How did you choose to react?

What was the outcome of the situation?

What lessons did you learn about yourself?

From that experience, how have you equipped yourself to handle future persecution?

What scriptures do you use to meditate on during times of persecution?

GROW

In patience.

We all know the adage "patience is a virtue", but do we practice this daily, or do we let our need to microwave everything get in our way? I believe the latter is the answer. I am an avid social media "scroller". I will stay up for hours scrolling through Facebook or Instagram looking at pictures, posts, and memes for inspiration or to get a feel for where our society is heading and without fail I usually come across topics speaking of relationships and having attained a certain status in life without putting in the work. It is easy to look at another person's life or in the case of social media, their posts and pictures and feel like they have it all and it came easily, but what we do not see is the real story. We do not see the struggle, pain, nor the highs and lows the person went through to get to point B. Being impatient is something that you must constantly keep at bay and remind yourself that whatever it is you are wanting will be, but sometimes that is not good enough. I would not be honest if I did not use myself as an example. I can be the most impatient person in the entire world when it comes to some things, but I am growing and that is why I have included this topic as a "grow". I know how to be patient for some things, but sometimes, I am in a hurry and it is usually the wrong thing, for example driving!

Driving literally stresses me out! I live 40 minutes from my place of employment on a good day, but on a bad day it takes me up to an hour and a half to get home. When I finally make it home, after looking for different routes or short cuts, my nerves are shot. Then, there is the snail drive who drives at least 10 miles below the speed limit and looks at you like you are the problem when you zoom around them…but let me move on because I can rest there the entire time. But, as I get older, I am becoming more patient, and that is a plus for me. One area I've grown to have patience is content in my singleness. I have not been in a "real" relationship in YEARS (and I put *real* in quotation marks because we all know that in this day and age, real relationships are far, few, and in between)! Although I have not been in a solid relationship, I have not rushed the ones I have been in to make them into something they were not, and this is what a lot of people do. People have a need to be with someone to share their life with and sometimes we choose to overlook the obvious and deal with toxicity and mess because we want something so bad. Then you have those who want success. They want to be the boss, run the company, have the good life but fail to understand that those things take time, effort, faith, perseverance, and dedication.

We see Reality TV stars pop on the scene and they "seem" to have it all. We have online bloggers and vloggers who pop on the scene and they too "seem" to have it all, but what we never get is the struggle before the victory, the success. You do not see the late nights and early mornings. You do not see what they must go without to make it to where they are. You only see the success, fame, good living and their dreams fulfilled. You see the outcome. You must change your mindset, because when you are patient, God is growing you. He is preparing you for obstacles and victories. He is setting the stage for your favor and protecting you along the way. In the waiting, there is growth, mentally, spiritually, and emotionally. I know firsthand the thoughts and craziness that takes place in the mind. As I said before, learning to be patient is an everyday task. Therefore, when I begin to lose hope in a dream, I meditate on the word and remind myself of Hannah and how the Lord blessed her womb, or think about how long it took Jacob to marry the woman his heart desired, and I find peace in knowing that God has my best at heart and when the time is right, I will have everything my heart desires and so will you! Do not speed up what God has been cultivating for you. Do not lean to your own understanding and forgo remaining faithful and trusting Him. Stay focused and be content where He has you until the time is right. Stop feeling the need to speed things up to get to the top. Stop looking for short-cuts and most importantly stop allowing people in your life that do not need to be there the opportunity to make you miss your true blessing. It is time to practice patience for it is surely a virtue!

Reflections:

What areas of your life are you lacking in patience?

Describe the outcomes resulting from your lack of patience.

What lessons did you learn when you were not patient?

Describe a time you were patient and how everything worked out for you.

What lessons did you learn from being patient?

What steps do you take to work on your patience?

Find 3-4 scriptures you can meditate on that will help you when you feel yourself becoming impatient with your progress or situation.

GROW

Stop constantly praying to receive from God.

I know you are thinking, "what in the world is she talking about?" But I am very serious! It is time to stop the repetitive continuous prayers asking God to give, give, give. Yes, I know the scriptures says to make your requests known to God, to ask and you shall receive and that He will bless you, BUT you must grow from that and truly understand that it is not all about ASKING to receive. God is not one to treat like a candy machine, putting your money (request) in to get a prize of candy in return. He is a gracious God. He is a loving God and He is your provider. It is time to learn to grow in your walk and prayer life. It is time to turn your prayers into submitting to His will. It is time to seek and meditate on His word to understand the blessings that come from it. You see being blessed is not just having material things or receiving things. It is honoring God by obeying His word and purpose for which you were born. It is walking in your purpose and being blessed with contentment and joy that you receive from fulfilling the thing for which you were born and from that, comes the blessings. From your obedience comes the desires of your heart, and from your relationship with God and honoring Him comes your blessings. I was once immature in my prayer life because I did not understand how to pray. As a child, I was taught the bedtime prayer without relationship and never questioned if there was more to it. I too, would always pray asking God to give, give, give, but something in me, the Holy Spirit, was nudging me on the inside saying that there is much more.

It was not until I earnestly sought God out and asked for Him to reveal Himself to me through His word that I began to understand how to pray and what it meant to ask Him for "things". I began to see that everything I am to have is already there for me.

It was not this magical prayer thing and voilà I received it. I began to understand that blessings and the things I receive come from spending time in His word and aligning my desires, wants, and needs to His. You see, praying for things you want is not always the things God wants for you and we should be careful when we go down that road. You must remember that God is always going to give you what you need, but when you continuously interject your prayers that are outside of His will, He will surely give you what you have asked for. You must know that our Father has your basic needs covered. If He provides for the birds in the air, what makes you think he will not provide those basic needs for you? You must grow to know that God is not a magic genie in a bottle and should never be treated in that manner. Growing and understanding the word of God for yourself is crucial and learning how to pray and talk to God is even more important. In all, you must look at your prayers like a conversation with God and allow the Holy Spirit to guide you and you will see your requests turn into you submitting more to God and his desires for you!

Reflections:

On a scale of 1-10, how strong is your prayer life?

How often do you find yourself praying for God to give you things?

What are your requests of God?

Which prayer requests are in accordance to His will?

Which prayer requests are not in accordance to His will?

Describe a time in which you prayed for a want? What happened? Did it turn out as expected? What did you learn from the experience?

Find 5-6 scriptures that speak of God's blessings. What common theme can be concluded?

Moving forward what steps can you take to grow your prayer life?

GROW

It is not about you! Put someone before yourself and pay it forward.

I think it is fair to say we live in a selfish, self-pleasing world. Now, I am not suggesting that you are part of the "it's all about me" clique, but in general there are a lot of individuals who are only concerned with their advancement and well-being. As a toddler, you live in the "me" stage for quite some time. Everything is "mine, mine, mine", and sharing is simply not an option. Toddlers are in a stage of exploration and do not understand the concept of sharing, which is why it is taught and it usually takes a few years for them to get an understanding as to what it means. Toddlers love attention and to be honest, do not know anything else, but that, because that is what we give them from the time they are born. So, when we begin to slowly burst their "it's all about me" bubble, it takes a few years to understand and learn how to share and care for someone else outside of their immediate family. But, as one gets older, you should begin to see that the world was not designed to revolve around you. You are simply not the bee's knees! I hate to crush your world, but as you grow, not just get older, but from a spiritual standpoint, you come to understand that you are not here to solely live for yourself and everything is not about you. As one matures in their spiritual walk, you begin to understand that you are here to aid others.

You are here to bless someone with what they need at the appointed time. You are here to teach someone a lesson you have learned to help them to not travel down the same road. You are here to give to those who are in need. You are here to encourage and motivate someone to reach for their goals, to live out their dreams, pursue their passion and walk in their purpose. You are here to care for those who cannot care for themselves or those who have no one to love and support them. You are here to minister to someone who needs an uplifting word to pull them out of the depths. You are here to bless someone, not for recognition or fame, but to pay it forward. You are here to be a testimony, to share your life's hardships and how you overcame to be an inspiration to the next person. We are not here to just live a good life, but a life with meaning lived unselfishly. We are to live a life in which you touch others with good intention. It is living a life that has a legacy and a story to tell of how you have reached others and left impressions of goodness on their lives. It is a life of seeing the need and meeting it! It is time to grow from a "me" state of mind, to a how can I "pay it forward" state of mind. It is time to seek opportunities to give back and make your mark on the world. It is time to stop living a life only focused on you, for it is a lonely life. It is time for you to reach out to others and make an impact on their life. It is time to pay it forward!

Reflections:

In your words define the term "selfish" and compare it to the dictionary's definition.

Do you see yourself as a "selfish" person per its definition? If you answered yes, list the areas in your life you are selfish with. If you answered no, please explain why you believe so.

Describe a situation in which you intentionally thought of someone else and paid it forward.

Describe how helping someone else made you feel.

Describe a time when someone paid it forward or thought of you and aiding you in a time of need.

Describe how the action made you feel.

Do you believe it is important to do for others outside of yourself? Explain why you believe so.

If you have not grown to a point of thinking and assisting others, what steps can you take to help move you in that directions?

GROW

In courage.

What is courage? Merriam-Webster's Dictionary defines courage as mental or moral strength to venture, persevere, and withstand danger, fear, or difficulty. Dictionary.com defines courage as the power or quality of dealing with or facing danger, fear, pain without fear; bravery. 2. Obsolete. The heart of the source of emotion. Lastly, Wikipedia defines courage in three ways- Courage, (also called bravery or valor) is the choice and willingness to confront agony, pain, danger, uncertainty, or intimidation. 2. Physical courage is facing physical pain, hardship, death, or threat of death and 3. Moral courage is the ability to act rightly in the face of popular opposition, shame, scandal, discouragement, or personal loss. As we grow in our spiritual walk we must grow in courage. As I review the definitions of courage, there is a running theme of danger, opposition, facing fears or difficult times and to me this suggest that this is something we must learn to do. Courage is embedded in us from birth, but is not activated until we need it. It lies dormant until it is time to birth it. Over the course of our lives we learn who we are and more importantly, who we are according to God. We begin to experience life and see it for what it is worth. We attach ourselves to other causes for the greater good and begin to challenge our thinking and motivation. Then without warning we encounter moments in our lives that birth courage.

These moments will arise and give you a sense of power like no other. It will challenge our sensibility and moral codes for what is right or wrong. It will lead us to take a stand. Exuding courage is an act of selflessness. It is standing up for a cause, a belief, or an idea. It is learning, in some situations and circumstances to put others before yourself to protect them. Having courage and displaying it is admirable. It shows strength and character. When I think of courage, the first thing that comes to my mind is "The Wizard of Oz". In the "The Wizard of Oz", there is a running theme of courage. We know about Lion who seemingly lacked courage and desired to be brave; but the other characters also displayed courage. Dorothy enters the Land of Oz, kills the Wicked Witch of the East, receives the ruby slippers and is pointed in the direction of the yellow brick road. Along the yellow brick road, she encounters the Scarecrow, Tin Man and the Lion, who are all looking to receive their desires from the Wizard. But, the Wizard sends them away to kill the Wicked Witch of the West before he grants them their desires. In doing so, we see them face multiple attacks along their journey to get what they desire. In the face of attack after attack, while using courage, they are receiving what they need and want. The Scarecrow wanted brains, but it was not until he was forced into a situation facing his fears that he "used" his brains to get him out of harm's way. Then you have the Tin Man, who so badly wanted a heart, but it was "heart" or courage that helped to defeat the opposition to get to Emerald City and defeat the Wicked Witch of the West and then we have the Lion.

The Lion's problem was that he did not believe he was brave. He did not feel he was strong to defeat his opponents, until he had a mission. To grow in courage, we are usually faced with a situation, a mission to do to overcome, but it is how we respond that determines if we have grown in courage. When we grow in courage, we simply stop looking at a situation as it only affecting us, and begin to see it as affecting the whole; and that is when we act. Courage requires the previous "Grow", helping others outside of ourselves to meet a need to change the course for someone else. It is deciding to use our moral compass despite the intimidation or ridicule we might experience. It is knowing that fear does not live in you. It is standing firmly, unashamed of the decisions you make to support or speak out against a cause. It is placing the need or life of someone else before yours, so that they may experience the greater. It is understanding that God will stand with you because you have chosen to stand with Him. Growing in courage is learning to be strong and unshakeable. Some great examples include, Dr. Martin L. King, Jr., Cesar Chavez, Harriet Tubman, John F. Kennedy, Abraham Lincoln, our service men and women who fight and protect our country daily, and from the bible, the Apostle Paul, the disciples and Jesus. These individuals encountered persecution, persevered, faced death or stood up against the opposition for the good of mankind; and that is the essence of courage! Soon there will come a time for you to stand on the shoulders of courage. Will you be ready?

Reflections:

Do you consider yourself a courageous person? Why? Why not?

Describe a time in which you activated courage in your life.

What was the result of your action?

Describe a time in which you chose not to be courageous.

What were your reasons for not doing so?

What causes will lead you to take a stand? Next to each cause, explain how you will exhibit courage.

GROW

By giving thanksgiving and praise in all circumstances.

Friday morning, I wake up to four missed calls from two doctors and three voice mail messages. My heart begins to pound, and my mind and flesh begin to take over by planting seeds of fear and uncertainty in my spirit. I listened to the voice messages all saying to call the doctor back as soon as possible. My results were in. It had been a week and now it was time to reveal what had been going on with me. For the past year, I had been experiencing more headaches, vertigo, nausea, being off balance, hand tremors and numbness in my lower extremities and feet. I had missed work it seemed every month and sleeping proved to be a challenge. I was gaining weight rapidly and it was placing me in a state of hopelessness, because no matter what I did, I never lost, only gained. Thursday evening, before the call, I was in Wal-Mart shopping and it felt like my spirit was being taken from me. With each step, walking became labored, the heart palpitations increased, and my vertigo was nonstop. I knew that I was going to pass out, but God! Right when I could no longer walk at a normal speed, my phone rang, and it was my best friend. I told her what was happening and if she did not hear from me in the next 30 minutes, I had probably fainted and would be at Wal-Mart. I quickly left and headed home. My mother suggested we go to the emergency room, but I was having no parts of that. The "spell" came again and I started experiencing hot flashes. I lied down and prayed. I prayed for God to heal me, to restore my body back to its normal state and I fell asleep. Now, here it is Friday morning and all I hear is urgency in the voices. I called the neurologist and I got the news. "Ms. Colston, we need to you make an appointment as soon as possible for a lumbar puncture. We are concerned because results show you have signs of intracranial pressure and we need to find out what the cause is."

My heart began to race. These terms were scaring me and

before I knew it, I was on the edge of panic, but the Holy Spirit stepped in and I pulled myself together. I began to calm down, although tears had formed in the corners of my eyes. I cleared my head and wrote down the information I was given and then called the other doctor. This called yielded more information about my diagnoses from lab results and I received it much better because it was on a list I had made as what was possibly wrong. The nurse read off my results which were arthritis of the neck, carpal tunnel, B1 deficient, intracranial pressure, and my TSH levels high and I wept, not because I was afraid, but because my prayers had been answered. I had received confirmation that it was not all in my head, that there was something wrong with my body as I had been saying for the last 5-6 years to no avail with other doctors. Now I had an answer. I had something to work from and I began to thank God and praise Him. I began to thank Him for not allowing me to give up. I began to thank Him for allowing my general practitioner to hear me and refer me to someone with more knowledge. I began to thank Him for allowing me to meet a doctor who was more concerned with getting to the truth, than just hustling patients in and out prescribing medications to band-aid the problems. I thanked God for hearing my cry and then I praised Him for being faithful! I praised Him for being my healer and victor! I praised Him for having my best interest at heart. There will be times when the world will seem to swallow you up with its many attacks, but in those situations, we must grow to learn that all will be well. We must learn to keep an attitude of positivity, because our natural reaction is one of negativity and pessimism. It took me a while to mature in this walk. I would receive "bad" news and cry and fret.

I would try to figure out how I could change it or what the "bad" outcome would result in. But, as I continued to read and grow in understanding, I began to realize that giving thanksgiving and praise in the face of dire situations or upsetting news is an intentional action. It is a conscious effort to see the positive and not be taken down the "rabbit hole" of negative emotions. Learning how to give thanksgiving and praise takes time and an intentional act of rewiring your brain to think in the positive. I remember when I used to get bad news and get scared. I would panic and work myself up into a frenzy about how things will transpire, not knowing I was already speaking against victory. But when I began to allow the Holy Spirit to guide my thoughts and actions, reside in me, and help push me through the hard times my reactions began to change. It will not be easy because your faith will be tested and meditating and arming yourself with scripture to speak to yourself in these times will be crucial. You will need to surround yourself with individuals who are strong in their faith and will be there for you to help direct your mind to the positive. You will need to arm yourself with scriptures to meditate on and bring to remembrance when the need arises. You will need to be intentional. When you mature in your spiritual walk, you understand how to give thanksgiving and praise. It is coming to know that when you praise and thank God, you are taking your eyes off the problem and placing it in His for Him to do the work. It is simply trusting God. Are you ready to get your shout on? Are you ready to see the end results? Are you ready to witness a miracle? If so, it is time to get your praise on!

Reflections:

When you receive unwanted or "bad" news, what is your initial reaction (s)?

Who do you share your news with? Are they strong in faith and do they pray for you or do they stay in the negative with you? How have they helped or hindered you?

Describe a situation where you saw the negative or no way out. What negative talk did you participate in? How long did you allow yourself to be sad, angry, or scared?

Do you feel you give thanksgiving and praises to God in all circumstances? If so, describe a time in which you received unwanted or bad news and could stand on the word of God.

If you are not mature in your walk to give thanksgiving and praise, explain the steps you will take to grow in this area of your spiritual growth.

GROW

Learn to live from the inside out!

Growing up is filled with tests and from those tests we learn how to handle situations as they arise. We begin to build a schema, a roller index if you will of life's situations and lessons learned that are meant to make us wiser in the future. One of those life's situations is when we are faced with adversaries, and when we are challenged by individuals who are sent to reveal our true nature and character. What do we do? Do we allow ourselves to sink to their level or do we rise above? I believe most of the time we sink to someone else's level and lose ground. A few years ago, my dad, Pastor Michael Colston, taught on living from the inside-out. He taught that we will always struggle with our flesh, because the flesh is self-seeking. It is not in alignment to God's word and does what it wants to do to feel good. He taught how we have two natures, one guided by the Holy Spirit and one led by the flesh and that in any given situation; we must decide which one we will allow to lead us. That sermon has stayed with me since. I remember the Monday after hearing it how I had to share it with someone at work. My coworker was upset with another coworker and was getting ready to lay in on her when I walked up to her and said "inside". She turned and looked at me quizzically. I pulled her to the side and explained that I knew she wanted to get some things off her chest, but was it what her spirit wanted or her flesh? She thought for a few seconds and said, her flesh. I went on to explain that when we get upset or frustrated with another person, our flesh will always want us to retaliate or attack to make it feel better, but that is not of God and not what Jesus would do. She nodded in agreement and said, "I like that, inside" and it became our thing. We would always see each other in the hall and anytime I seemed stressed or upset, she would whisper "inside", and I to her.

Living from the inside is what Jesus did during his 33 years.

He chose to not allow what was going on against him to affect His responses. He was persecuted. Lied on. Betrayed. Mocked. Ridiculed and never reacted in the same nature. When we live from the inside-out, we are choosing to rise above allowing the Holy Spirit to guide our actions. We are choosing to not conform or be tempted into the same actions of another, even if everyone is reacting the same way. Simply put, living from the inside is walking in the ways of Christ and obeying the word of God. It is choosing to not hold contempt for another in your heart. It is refusing to hold on to grudges. It is choosing to remain in peace and not allowing someone to steal your joy. It is acknowledging the action or attack and responding with grace and love. Choosing to live from the inside-out is an intentional and a daily decision. I used to be quick of the tongue. I could give a lashing and move on feeling great about myself, but as I matured in my spiritual growth, I began to feel guilty and prayed for God to tame my mouth. I now wait before responding. I assess my feelings and pray and ask God to help me to discern what is truly going on. I make conscious decisions daily to live from the inside. Will living from the inside be an easy task? No, because it goes against our sin nature, our flesh. But when you choose to live from the inside, when you give it try, when you choose to be free from your flesh, you will see that living from the inside is a stress-less life and going back to the former will be out of the equation!

Reflections:

How do you react when placed in a trying situation?

What happens to your body when you become upset?

What are the results of your actions?

What would you need to begin learning how to live from the inside-out?

Who can be your accountability partner to help you in this area?

What does living from the inside look like for you?

Find 5-6 scriptures to aid you in growing in this area?

GROW

In peace.

When the spirit placed this on me, I did not know what direction to take. I did not know if I should speak from a standpoint of allowing peace to reside in you, meaning not to allow outside circumstance to disrupt you by remaining calm, tranquil; or to remain silent, quiet. The more I thought on it and looked at the definition and scriptures, the more I was led to encourage you to allow peace to reside in you when surrounded by the craziness of this world, and when your life seems upside down. Peace is something I believe we all want. We want to have this feeling on the inside that is calm under pressure and releases to us strength to withstand anything that comes against us. Psalm 29:11 says, "The Lord will give strength to His people; The Lord will bless His people with peace." This peace of calmness and no strife is what we all desire. When we allow circumstances and situations to overrule us, we lose peace. We lose our ground to stand on to combat it because we become frazzled and worried. One cannot worry and have peace at the same time. When we worry, we are saying we do not trust that God has our back. We work ourselves up, disrupt our thought process and we hurt ourselves internally, because worrying causes harm to our bodies. Living in peace is doing as Philippians 4:6-7 says, "be anxious for nothing, but in everything by prayer and supplication, with thanksgiving, let your requests be made known to God; and the peace of God, which surpasses all understanding will guard your hearts and minds through Christ Jesus. Growing in peace is giving it up to God! Residing in peace is walking with God and allowing him to guard and protect you, especially our minds, for this is where the battlefield is. My growth in peace came my senior year in high school. A young man approached me one day and asked for my number. I did not give it to him and from that day forward he would show up at my locker and ask for it or ask to walk me to my classes. It got so bad that other young men in my classes or who knew me would walk with me or stand up for me.

Then one night it all came to a head, after repeatedly calling my house and hanging up or standing and staring at me at school, he threw a cocktail bomb at my house and it was one of the scariest things that ever happened to me. That night the peace in our home was disrupted and would remain so for the remainder of the year. Being stalked was one on the worst experiences of my life. I was scared and nervous all the time. I was constantly watching my back and it drove my dad to a dark place. I remember being afraid to talk to boys from that point on because I did not know how me not being interested in them would turn out. I was unsettled but pressed on with a strong, fake front. No one in my school, besides my principal knew what was going on. I was stressed out and had no peace. I learned to fake being happy and resilient around my friends and family, but inside I was angry, depressed, and scared. I was not strong in the word, and found myself praying for harm to come to the stalker. I do not remember if I told my mother this, but I do remember her giving me a scripture, Psalm 118:6, "The Lord is on my side; I will not fear. What can man do to me?" This scripture saved me. It gave me instant peace and security. I was no longer going to allow this person to define my world and dictate my movements. I was no longer going to give in to fear or praying for harm to come his way. I gave it to God. The young man eventually left me alone and all the people he got involved in harassing me at school and in my work place sent me apologies. In that moment, I knew God was real to me. That experience awakened my spirit man and I have never been the same. Today I walk in peace. I refuse to allow other people to steal it from me. I guard my heart and mind with the word and pray for God to keep me by thanking Him for His peace daily. I use discernment in situations and am mindful of others who seek to destroy my peace. Growing in peace is an intentional decision as well. We can choose to continuously allow situations to shake us up or we can choose to stand strong, pray and allow the Lord to take over. The decision is yours!

Reflections:

What does peace look like to you?

Describe a time when your peace was disrupted?

How was peace restored and what lessons did you learn about yourself?

Are you functioning in peace? If you are, explain how. If you are not, explain why.

What current situation in your life may threaten to disrupt your peace?

How can you practice walking in peace?

What 4 scriptures can you use to center your spirit back to peace?

GROW

In your spiritual walk.

Do you remember the first time you attended church? I know I do not, but what I do remember is attending church as a child. I remember going to Sunday school before church started and being taught different lessons from the bible. I remember going to alter call trying to figure out why we were up there and why everyone was repeating this song, "Bread of Heaven, which I never knew the words to. I remember women shouting and passing out and thinking to myself how funny it was and why it was happening. I remember on certain Sundays how certain women would wear white and sit on the front row. I remember the pastor saying a few things and then begin to breathe funny and make annoying noises. I remember the feeling I had that led me to accept Jesus as my savior and was baptized. I remember these things from my early childhood, but I do not remember any specific word taught that formed a deep relationship or desire to want to learn more. I remember telling my father that I was not understanding and that led to him looking for another church home for us to grow. He indeed stayed true to his word of ensuring we (his children) learned and understood the word of God and he was led to Oak Cliff Bible Fellowship. Here was the place. This was where I began to grow spiritually by being taught, not preached to. I was learning more about God and His grace. I began to understand who Jesus was and my desire to want to understand the bible grew stronger and stronger. My moral compass changed, and I pledged to myself to live a life pleasing to the Lord. I learned how to pray and would pray for God to reveal His word to me, to make it alive in me. Dr. Evans's teaching grew me, but I was still missing that knowledge and knowing for myself and King James was not helping me at all. Then one day it happened!

I opened the bible after many years of praying and the word illuminated. I saw it clearly and understood it. I began to apply it and use it to help me grow me spiritually and in doing this, a struggle started in my body between my flesh and spirit that I had not been aware of before. When I was an infant, a babe on milk in Christ, I did not struggle between doing right by the Lord. I did what felt right to me and that was not operating in the spirit, but as I began to grow in understanding the word pierced my heart and I moved from milk to meat. I began praying for others, speaking life into others and lived my life the best I could without staying in a carnal frame of mind. To grow, I had to do a few things that required dealing with my flesh. I do not know what your complete journey to spiritual growth will look like but here are three key steps in my journey that led me to where I am now. The first step to spiritual growth is submission. You must submit yourself to God for Him to affect your heart. You must come under the word of God and examine your way of life to align it with the life God wants for you. You do this by submitting to His will and allowing the word of God to be your compass. Next, admission of sins and your truths need to take place. You must face your sins and repent. By acknowledging your truths, examining your ways, and confessing your sins you can begin to work through them with God's help to conquer them. You will find that you are no longer facing them with your strength, but with the guidance of the Holy Spirit. Finally, there is denial. Denial is crucial. A lot of Christians will submit, accept, and admit their sins, but there is a majority who will not deny their flesh and rest in living as a carnal Christian. You cannot be carnal and grow in your walk at the same time. You must be all in. You must realize that we are beings that consist of a body, spirit, and soul.

Our body is in the business of seeking pleasure and living how it wants to live. When you feed the body and never feed the spirit what it wants you to begin to die spiritually and your soul (intellect), mind, will rest in carnality. When you begin to grow in your spiritual walk, denying your flesh will be a daily task. In 1 Corinthians 15:3, Paul tells the church of Corinth, "I die daily", meaning he dies daily to the wants of "self" and lives his life in accordance to what God wants. Is growing spiritually going to be easy, no, of course not? It will require you to change your mind as Paul writes in Romans 12:1-2 that you must "be transformed by the renewing of your mind, so that you may prove what the will of God is, that which is good and acceptable and perfect". It will test you and you will fail several times, but because you are growing, you know that God's grace is sufficient and will carry you through. As I started this section, I mentioned that growing up is an essential part of life. It is something we cannot bypass in life, but being grown is a totally different thing, just as growing in your faith is. You can believe in the Lord and trust that Christ will keep you, but if you are not willing to let your heart be infected with the word and walk in that, there will be no growth. Remember in the beginning, how I said I went to church as a kid, but did not have the relationship, which meant I was not growing spiritually; but as I continued to grow physically my spiritual needs grew and I stayed steadfast in maturing in my walk. If you are not there yet, keep growing. Keep reading and seeking God for you. Keep growing spiritually for your growth is centered in Christ. Allow the Holy Spirit to guide you, pray for illumination of the word, and find a leader who will teach you the word so that it may become real to you. It is time for you to do the basic three: submit, admit, and deny your flesh so that you can grow and walk in the will of God.

Reflections:

What does spiritual growth mean to you?

Where do you consider yourself on the spectrum of spiritual growth: infant, adolescent, or adult? Explain why?

If you are growing in your walk, list the steps you have taken to grow.

How has your life changed since focusing on growing spiritually?

How do you handle the crises of life now?

If you are not growing, list the steps you must take and things you must give up to be successful.

Who can be your accountability partner in supporting you with your spiritual growth?

Find 5 scriptures that speak of spiritual growth and meditate on them and ask the Holy Spirit to reveal its meaning to you. Here are two to start:

1 Peter 2:2- What is this verse saying?

Hebrew 5: 12-14- What are these verses saying?

GROW

In your abilities.

Each person on this planet is born with a talent. Yes, you have a natural talent. This talent was formed in you during your formative months in the womb and has been cultivated as you have grown. For just a moment, I want you to think about what you can do better than someone else, what you are good at doing or something that seems to just come naturally for you without a lot of work. Do you have it in mind? If so, that is your talent. Now the question becomes what are you going to do with it? Before we go further, let me clarify spiritual gifts from talents. Spiritual gifts are given to us when we choose to come under the word of God and allow the Holy Spirit to work in us. Our spiritual gifts increase as we mature in our walk and develop a deeper relationship with God. Spiritual gifts are not easily recognizable, and you cannot improve them on your own; God does that. With natural talents, you can improve it and choose to use it for the world or to glorify God. But spiritual gifts are only used to serve God's purposes and to uplift the body of Christ. I know that most of my spiritual gifts shocked me. I know many do not believe in the gift of speaking in tongues, but that one scared me!

It came upon me or rather out of me during a period of fasting and praying. I was lying prostrate on the floor praying and praising God when a sequence of words flowed out of my mouth that I did not recognize, and it scared me. I opened my eyes and looked around the room and noticed how warm I was on the inside and that I was crying uncontrollably. I was thinking maybe I just heard myself wrong…just maybe, but as I went back into prayer and opened my mouth the same sequence of words flowed out again, and I could not stop until the Holy Spirit was done with me. I was afraid to share this because I knew how a lot of Christians looked upon it as not real or people do it just for "play", but to believe the bible in its entirety is to believe everything and being gifted in tongues is real. But when I look back at my natural talent for writing, it did not shock me, but others. Natural talents do not shock us because we know it is something we can do. We can easily identify natural talent in others and stand in awe when we see a person using them. We can even try to predict what talents a child might have when they are born based off of their parents or generational history, but that does not mean people will use them.

Sometimes we get scared of our spiritual gifts or natural talents and do nothing with them. We do not exercise and flow in our abilities because we are usually afraid of not being successful, but that is the lie of the enemy. When we do not use our gifts or talents they will atrophy, just as our limbs do when we do not use them. I am reminded of the parable found in Matthew 25:14-30. This parable speaks of how a master gives his servants different amounts of talents according to their *ability* and leaves for some time. As he is away, the servants are able to do as they please. The master gave five to one, two to another and one to his last servant. The servants who received more went out and gained more, but the servant who received one, hid his in the ground. Does this sound familiar? Do you know people who use their talents and gifts and things in their life begin to multiple? Of course, you do! Just as you know individuals who have gifts and talents who never use them, and they spend their life feeling as if they do not measure up. But it is a choice.

When the master returns he gives the servants who have used their talents more and the one who hid his talent was taken away. It is time to grow in your abilities. It is time to do more! It is time to find your way and use what God has formed in you and has given to you. Stop being afraid of the "what if's"! Stop being afraid of people's opinions! Stop telling yourself you are not good enough! Trust me when I say do it! Do what you were born to do and use it for the good of others, not just yourself. Share your talents and gifts and watch them multiply! Know that you are better than good enough! Know that you are successful! Know that by doing what you were born to do, you will experience peace and joy! As Pastor Mike Colston always says "What's in your hand?" What has God given to you that is your way out! What has God anointed you with? It's time to grow those abilities! No more holding back! Go. Do. Bless. Be as Success!

Reflections:

Make a list of your natural talents.

Which talents do you use daily and which have you buried deep within?

What is stopping you from using your talent(s)?

How are you growing in your talent(s)?

How would you like to use your talent(s)? (for the world or God)

What are your spiritual gifts? (If you do not know pray and ask God to reveal them to you)

How are you using your spiritual gift(s)?

What shocked or scares you the most about your spiritual gift(s)?

How can you use your spiritual gift(s) to glorify God?

How can you use your talent(s) and spiritual gift(s) to bless others and to glorify God?

GROW

In obedience.

As you grow in your spiritual walk, you will learn that being obedient to God's word is a must. As Christians, our growth is tied to being obedient. We are obedient when we hear the word, receive it from the Holy Spirit and take action. A lot of Christians are not obedient the first time God speaks to us. It may take weeks, months or years for us to do the will of God, but guess what, the word He gave us never changes. I know that in the past, God gave me many opportunities to do and take action, but I was allowing fear of my accomplishments and the work that it would take to get it done to hold me back. I never for one moment during those times told God my fears so that he could address them. I simply made one step in the direction and when I was faced with difficulties and hardships, I allowed the God-given word to go by the wayside. For whatever the reason, we hold ourselves back from being obedient. We create scenarios in our mind and allow negative self-talk to talk us out of doing the will of God. Let's take a look at two examples in the bible. In Genesis, God gives directions to Eve to eat from every tree in the garden except the one tree in the middle (Gen. 3:1-2), but Eve disobeyed God due to the deception of the serpent. The lesson here is that when we are given directions by God, we must not be led astray by the shiny, feel good, attractive outer appearance of the world; or heed the voice of those who do not want us to succeed.

We must be diligent in protecting our minds and tune out the static that wants to cause interference. In Genesis 6-9, we learn about Noah. Sometimes obeying God, will cause us to look insane to others. Outsiders will not understand our motives or actions and will call you all types of names, but you must not let that deter you. You must stay focused and complete what has been assigned to you because from it you will reap the harvest, promise, success and great accomplishments that await you at the end. Noah was instructed by God to build an ark because He was going to cause a great flood to destroy all humanity for the earth was displeasing to God. Not once did Noah question God. Not once did Noah believe he was unfitting to do the will of God. Noah simply obeyed the instructions God had given him. I am sure Noah had no idea what an ark was, and I am sure, he had seen rain, but did not comprehend the idea of a flood covering earth to lead to extinction, but nevertheless, he completed what God instructed him to do. These are just two examples in the bible, but it is filled with many.

What you will learn is that being obedient to God will not be without challenges. It will not be easy street and you will have to stay focused, faithful and be fearless in doing the will of God. Growing in obedience will require fellowship with God meditating on the word and praying so that you can clearly hear Him. It will push you in ways that you have not been pushed before and it will be unsettling. It will require you to trust God with all things and know that His directions are fool-proof and will not fail you as Numbers 23:19 says, "God in not a man, that he should tell or act a lie, neither the son of man, that He should feel repentance. Has He said and shall He not do it? Or has He spoken and shall He not make it good?" It will require you to make changes in your life that you had not planned on. It will cause people to distance themselves or leave you altogether. It will cause a range of emotions, but through it all you will not be alone. You will be led by the Holy Spirit and protected by the blood of Jesus. You will work hard and get discouraged, but do not become weary in doing good, (Gal. 6:9), instead lean on Jesus, call on His strength and press your way. It is time to step out on faith, heed the word of God and DO!

Reflections:

What has God placed on your heart to do?

What led or hindered you in obeying God?

Obeying God comes with some challenges, what were your challenges and how did you overcome them?

What range of emotions did you experience?

What are some examples of negative self-talk you often partake in?

What were the results of obeying or disobeying God's word?

Who are you MOST like in the bible when it comes to obeying the word of God? Why?

Find 3-4 scriptures to motivate you when God gives you a task to complete.

~Prayer~

Dear Heavenly Father, I come to you thanking you for this word of Growth. Lord forgive me for not growing in the word as I should. I know that at times I have chosen to allow the world to take my attention from you, but I pray that I will begin to reconnect to form a deeper and more personal relationship with you. Father, I thank you for your son Jesus Christ who died on the cross just for me. I thank You that His blood covers me and that the gift of the Holy Spirit guides me. Lord, I pray that You will clear out the noise and allow me to only hear your voice. I pray that I will begin to grow in your word and live out that which You have already predestined for me. Lord, help me to see myself as you see me and build up my faith in You. I give myself to You Father God to do as you please. I am Yours and You are mine Lord. I praise You for Your holiness, grace, love, kindness, omnipresence, mercy, blessings and protection. I praise You for not being done with me yet! I praise You for the change in me that will align me to Your will and ways. Lord, I thank you, lift Your name up on high and will forever proclaim Your magnificence. In Jesus's name, I solemnly pray! Amen!

~Affirmation~

Lord, I declare that I will grow in YOU! I will submit to your will and way! I will use the Holy Spirit as my guide and begin to live from the inside-out. I will not allow the enemy to overtake my mind and control my actions towards others. I will be mindful of my ways and character for I am a child of God. I am a victor and your word will sustain me. I am set apart for your purpose and I will walk and honor who I am in you! I will be obedient to your word and will tune my ear and inner man to your voice. I will use my God given talents and gifts to glorify your name and I will not be a victim of fear! I will shower you with thanksgiving and praise and bless your holy name for you are the Alpha and Omega, the beginning and the end! I will walk in patience and be courageous to stand for You! I will live in peace and be mindful of the tactics of the enemy! I am a victor! I am blessed! I am prosperous! I have all authority in me to call on the name of Jesus who shall set me free from fear! I am courageous! I am called for a special purpose and I claim my position. I will grow! I will mature in my walk! I will make intentional connections with you! I say Yes to you Lord! I honor you Father and sing praises to Your sweet name for in You is the spring of life!

NOTES

CPSIA information can be obtained
at www.ICGtesting.com
Printed in the USA
BVOW11s1513070518
515517BV00001B/8/P

9 781973 617389